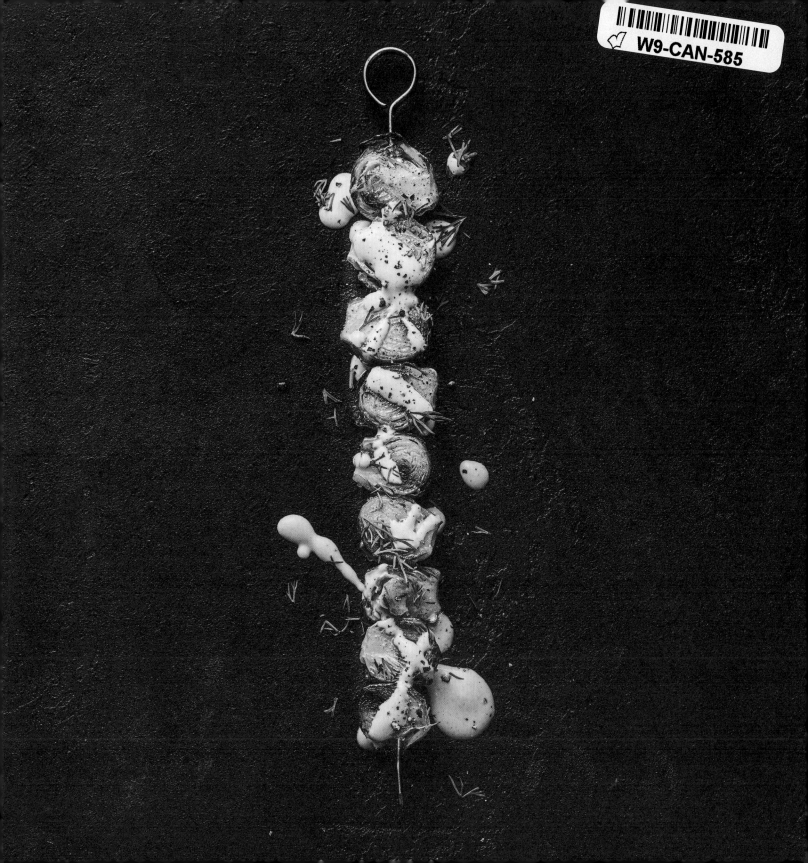

FLAVOR for ALL

To our babies, Parker Lee and August, and your big appetites! This is for you. Love, Mom and Dad

FLAVOR for ALL

EVERYDAY
RECIPES

CREATIVE
PAIRINGS

JAMES BRISCIONE and
BROOKE PARKHURST

Photography by Andrew Purcell

HOUGHTON MIFFLIN HARCOURT

Boston New York 2020

CONTENTS

Introduction | 1

Ingredients | 6

FLAVOR PAIRING , IN 500 WORDS
OR LESS | 6

FAT | 7

ACID/SOUR | 9

SALT | 10

UMAMI | 10

BITTER | 11

SWEET | 11

VEGETABLES 13

18 UMAMI IN A BOTTLE
lettuce, mustard, fennel, vinegar

19 COCO-SLAW *coconut milk, cabbage,
cilantro, carrot*

20 GRILLED LEEKS VINAIGRETTE
*allium, mushrooms, almonds, feta,
tarragon*

22 AVOCADO TOAST *avocado, fennel,
apple, cocoa, ancho chile*

25 AVOCADO "SUCCOTASH" *avocado,
corn, tomato, basil*

27 ROASTED BEET SALAD
beet, orange, mint, hazelnuts, yogurt

28 A DIFFERENT KIND OF GREEN
SALAD *cucumber, melon, jalapeño*

31 WATERMELON BRUSCHETTA
watermelon, tomato, pecorino

33 SICILIAN-STYLE PEACH SALAD
peach, fennel, olives, mint, chile

34 BRUSSELS SPROUTS KEBABS
brussels sprouts, chipotle chile, yogurt, dill

37 ASPARAGUS AND POTATO CHIP
GRATIN *asparagus, potato chips,
mushrooms*

39 CAESAR ARTICHOKE DIP
artichoke, anchovy, lemon

40 WHOLE ROASTED CAULIFLOWER
cauliflower, mustard, citrus

42 BROCCOLI WITH PISTACHIO PESTO
broccoli, pistachios, basil

43 EGGPLANT DIP *yogurt, dill, sesame, pomegranate, eggplant*

44 SQUASH SKEWERS *squash, bacon, carrot, vinegar*

46 PUMPKIN PILAF *jalapeño, cinnamon, fennel seeds, pumpkin*

47 SCALLOPED PARSNIPS *parsnip, lemon, cream*

49 SUMMER SQUASH GRATIN *squash, tomato, mint, ricotta*

Grains and Pasta | 50

52 SPRING VEGETABLE, BROWN BUTTER, AND LEMON PASTA *brown butter, peas, lemon*

55 CREAMED KALE AND CARAMELIZED ONION MAC AND CHEESE *pasta, kale, caramelized onion*

59 RIGATONI ALLA GRICIA WITH MUSHROOM "PANCETTA" *mushrooms, maple syrup, soy sauce, vinegar*

61 QUINOA SALAD *hazelnuts, vinegar, sweet potato, honey*

63 FARRO AND CRISPY KALE SALAD *wheat, bell pepper, tomato, feta*

67 SUMMER SQUASH VONGOLE *squash, clams, tomato, basil*

68 SWEET PEA AND MUSHROOM RIGATONI CARBONARA *eggs, sweet peas, mushrooms, wheat*

70 VEGETABLE BOLOGNESE WITH OLIVE GREMOLATA *olives, sage, orange, almonds*

Cheese | 72

74 CHERRY-OLIVE JAM *cherries, olives, wine*

75 BUFFALO CAULIFLOWER BAKE *cauliflower, blue cheese*

77 CRANBERRY-STUFFED BAKED BRIE *dairy, cranberries, orange*

79 ULTIMATE GRILLED CHEESE SANDWICHES *cheese, bread*

80 SPICY KIWI AND BACON GRILLED CHEESE SANDWICHES *kiwi, jalapeño, bacon*

82 BROCCOLI AND KIMCHI GRILLED CHEESE SANDWICHES *kimchi, broccoli, cheddar*

83 HAM AND APPLE GRILLED CHEESE SANDWICHES *olives, apple, pork*

84 ULTIMATE BLT WITH "TO-MAYO" *bacon, tomato*

87 FRICO, AKA CRISPY CHEESE CAKES *broccoli rabe, cheese, onion*

LAND
91

Chicken | 92

95 SPICY POMEGRANATE AND CHICKEN LETTUCE WRAPS *chicken, pomegranate, chile, lemongrass*

96 PAN-ROASTED CHICKEN WITH CREAMED GREENS AND POTATOES *chicken, mustard greens, cream, lemon*

99 PAN-SEARED CHICKEN WITH HERBED CARROTS AND MUSTARD *dill, butter, lemon, carrot*

101 ULTIMATE HONEY-MUSTARD CHICKEN *yogurt, mustard, basil, honey*

102 SOUTHWESTERN GRILLED CHICKEN SALAD *grapes, corn, tomato, cilantro*

103 CREAMY TOMATO CHICKEN RAGU *tomato, cream, onion, vodka*

107 GINGER BEER–BATTERED CHICKEN FINGERS *ginger beer, lime, chili powder*

108 INDIAN CHICKEN AND GREEN VEGETABLE PILAU *green peas, cucumber, hazelnuts*

Beef, Pork, and Lamb | 110

112 SLOW COOKER SWEET POTATO AND ALE BEEF STEW *sage, sweet potato, beer*

115 PAN-SEARED BEEF WITH BOURBON-RAISIN SAUCE *raisins, bourbon, mustard, worcestershire*

117 SEARED STEAKS WITH ALMOND-CHERRY PESTO *almonds, garlic, oregano, cherry*

119 GRILLED BEEF AND EGGPLANT WITH ESPRESSO BUTTER *beef, eggplant, espresso*

122 CHIANTI-BRAISED BEEF WITH GRITS *red wine, corn, butter*

Pork | 126

127 GRILLED PORK WITH SPICY PINEAPPLE AND BASIL RELISH *pork, pineapple, basil*

131 PAN-SEARED PORK MEDALLIONS WITH APPLES, BALSAMIC VINEGAR, AND BOURBON *coffee, balsamic vinegar, apple, bourbon*

133 SLOW COOKER PORK WITH MUSTARD, ORANGE, AND SAGE *mustard, orange, sage*

134 APPLE-BRINED PORK WITH CARAMELIZED ONION AND BOURBON GRAVY *apple, pork, bourbon, onion*

136 BROWN BUTTER, MAPLE, AND PEAR PORK ROAST *pear, pork, maple*

Lamb | 138

139 BRAISED LAMB WITH BLUE CHEESE AND MUSHROOM-POTATO GRATIN *lamb, blue cheese, mushrooms, potato, brandy*

141 BRAISED LAMB WITH SPICY PEACH CHUTNEY *corn, peaches, grenache wine*

144 ROAST LAMB AND CARROTS WITH MINT AND LEMON *carrot, mint, lemon, garlic*

145 HORSERADISH AND CITRUS-CRUSTED LAMB ROAST *lamb, orange, basil, horseradish*

146 GRILLED LAMB WITH ANCHOVY VINAIGRETTE *lamb, radish, anchovy, lettuce*

SEA 149

Fish | 150

153 PAN-SEARED FISH WITH BROCCOLI *breadcrumbs, broccoli, balsamic vinegar*

155 FISH WITH BACON AND CREAMY TOMATO FARRO *tomato, farro, bacon, cream*

156 FISH WITH LEMON-DILL LETTUCE SAUTÉ *fish, lettuce, lemon, dill*

158 MILK-POACHED FISH WITH BASIL *fish, milk, onion, basil*

161 PAN-SEARED FISH WITH BROWN BUTTER AND GRAPE VINAIGRETTE *brown butter, fennel, grapes*

162 MISO AND MAPLE-GLAZED FISH *maple syrup, miso, vinegar*

163 FISH WITH SWEET PEA AND HAM QUINOA PILAF *peas, mushrooms, ham*

165 FENNEL-SEARED FISH WITH GREEN BEANS, SESAME, AND DILL *fennel, green beans, sesame, dill*

167 FISH WITH SWEET POTATO-POBLANO HASH *sweet potato, mushrooms, basil, honey, mustard*

168 FISH WITH SPICED POTATOES AND AVOCADO CREAM *potato, tomato, avocado*

Shrimp, Crab, and Lobster | 170

171 CHILLED CARROT SOUP WITH POACHED SHRIMP *carrot, ginger, red wine*

174 CREAMY SHRIMP PASTA WITH CHARRED TOMATO AND PUMPKIN *shrimp, pumpkin, cream, bread, pasta*

176 BRAZILIAN SHRIMP AND COCONUT STEW *shrimp, tomato, coconut, pepper*

179 LUMP CRAB BRUSCHETTA *tomato, sesame, dill, toast*

180 CRAB AND CRISP APPLE SALAD *apple, mayonnaise, chive, lime*

181 GRILLED LOBSTER AND BUTTERNUT SQUASH WITH TOMATO, OLIVE, AND PRESERVED LEMON RELISH *lobster, butternut squash, olive, tomato*

DRINKS 183

185 COCOA AND LEMON OLD FASHIONED *cocoa, whiskey, lemon*

186 SPICED BUTTERNUT SQUASH OLD FASHIONED *bourbon, butternut squash*

187 MEZCAL MICHELADA *mezcal, beer, coriander*

189 GRAPEFRUIT ROSEMARY SPRITZ *grapefruit, gin, aperol*

190 CUCUMBER, APPLE, AND SAUVIGNON BLANC SANGRIA *cucumber, sauvignon blanc wine, grapes, apple*

192 PEACH, BASIL, AND ROSÉ SANGRIA *basil, peach, lime, rosé wine*

195 RASPBERRY-VANILLA SODA *vanilla, raspberry, thyme*

196 GRAPEFRUIT SHRUB *grapefruit, honey, vinegar*

198 SPICY PEACH SODA *peach, chile, ginger*

199 HOMEMADE COLA *citrus, star anise, cinnamon, mint*

BAKED 201

204 WALNUT AND OLIVE FOCACCIA
olives, walnuts, rosemary

207 CHERRY TOMATO AND NECTARINE
CROSTATA *cherry tomato, nectarine,
balsamic vinegar, mint*

209 NUTTY BETTER COOKIES
peanuts, fish sauce, cayenne

211 BOURBON, PECAN, AND COFFEE
SWEET ROLLS *bourbon, pecans, coffee*

213 TROPICAL CARAMEL UPSIDE-DOWN
CAKE *citrus, banana, pineapple, caramel*

214 SWEET-AND-SOUR PLUM UPSIDE-
DOWN CAKE *orange, honey, vinegar,
cornmeal*

216 SPICY CHOCOLATE CRINKLE
COOKIES *chile, coffee, cocoa*

217 "LIME AND THE COCONUT"
POPCORN MOUSSE *popcorn, coconut,
lime*

219 CARROT CAKE CRÈME BRÛLÉE
carrot, walnuts

221 RHUBARB WITH BOURBON
ZABAGLIONE *rhubarb, bourbon*

223 NOT-THAT-KIND-OF-MUSHROOM
BROWNIES *mushrooms, cocoa*

225 "THE KING" OF BROWNIES
peanut butter, banana, chocolate

228 BROWN BUTTER–ESPRESSO CARROT
CAKE *walnuts, espresso, carrot*

229 BROWN BUTTER ICE CREAM SUNDAE
brown butter, vanilla

232 NUTELLA AND BROWN BUTTER
SQUASH PANINI *vanilla, squash, nutella*

233 CHOCOLATE AND RED WINE BREAD
PUDDING *merlot wine, chocolate, whiskey*

236 VERNACCIA-POACHED PEARS WITH
PECORINO *vernaccia wine, pear, pecorino*

Index | 240

INTRODUCTION

For both of us, sharing our previous book, *The Flavor Matrix,* was an incredible journey. James created an exceptional reference book that is recognized as much for its innovation as for its thought-provoking graphics. In it, he distilled the complex chemistry of flavor and gave everyone a lesson in food pairing. We were surprised and excited by the diversity of readers drawn to the book: food geeks, culinary students, dialed-in soccer moms, mixologists, and "weekend warriors." No matter their background, they often asked us the same question: "How do you cook at home?"

> That oft-repeated question inspired us to write this book, an index of no-fail, kick-ass, chemistry-enabled recipes for everyday cooking.

While we are always thinking about how flavors and pairings can make every meal as delicious as possible, the reality is,

we're busy. We have a new restaurant. We have two young children at home. We have around one hour at the end of the day to make something tasty for dinner. That means that every dish on our table cannot be a deeply researched masterpiece. The flavor matrixes are always in our heads, but we also have a "cheat sheet" of greatest hits.

Sometimes a subtle twist on a classic or a gentle pop of unexpected flavor is enough. The recipes in *Flavor for All* reflect our simple, thoughtful, flavor-focused approach to home cooking. They're deeply delicious, yet easy; unexpected, but still familiar. Dishes such as Asparagus and Potato Chip Gratin (page 37); Fish with Bacon and Creamy Tomato Farro (page 155); and Chocolate and Red Wine Bread Pudding (page 233).

And we never ignore the classics. *The Flavor Matrix* revealed why some of our favorite flavor combinations—think cheese pizza, or pork chops and applesauce—work so well together. Margherita pizza contains the compound 4-methylpenta-noic acid, a chemical commonality among cheese, tomato sauce, and baked wheat that serves to enhance the flavor of all three when combined. In the pairing of pork and apples, 2-acteylfuran is one of the compounds that links this classic combination together. You always knew that these dishes tasted great, and *The Flavor Matrix* helps you understand why.

Flavor for All, in turn, builds on the science behind some of these classic combinations and fine tunes the techniques and ingredients to create more than 100 epic recipes.

For example, as a variation on the aforementioned pork and apple pairing, we've included a recipe for Apple-Brined Pork with Caramelized Onion and Bourbon Gravy (page 134). The compound we mentioned, 2-acetylfuran, is not only found in pork and apples but is also prevalent in bourbon and alliums. This recipe kicks off with a simple brine made from items you already have in your fridge or pantry—apple juice, soy sauce, and mustard—so you can mix it up before work or school and be ready to cook the juiciest, most flavorful pork you've ever tasted as soon as you get home.

Flavor for All is a book about how we live—to eat! We are working parents first, food- and wine-obsessed innovators second. We want this book to be functional, fun, and indispensable. The breakdown of the book is just like us: simple and focused on the food. We begin with a brief introduction to review the concept of flavor pairing and to set the scene for the recipes to come.

Next, we originally wanted to create a section of the book that would act as a culinary cheat sheet—something that could help new and experienced cooks alike understand how to build maximum flavor into every single dish they prepare. This next-level approach is something James has taught to cooks around the world through his role as the director of culinary research at the Institute of Culinary Education and now as a Food Network personality. Whether it's about how proteins react to salt, the right way to boil an egg, or the proper technique behind a perfect bowl of spaghetti, this insider knowledge will make everyone a more confident and capable cook. Then we decided not to do that.

Instead, we took those nuggets of culinary wisdom gained over a lifetime in the kitchen and put them where they would be most useful: in the recipes themselves. All of *our* best-loved cookbooks are full of handwritten notes in the margins—helpful reminders, or brief explanations of why something is done a specific way. We love those little margin notes, so we decided to go ahead and create them for you—right there in the margins as if you had written them yourself. It's our way of saying, "Hey, here's something you should know about this recipe" without interrupting the cooking process. These notes range from the science behind what is happening in a particular step of the recipe to gentle reminders about basic technique.

Beyond the science of cooking, we also wanted to pull the curtain back on the theory of taste development. Creating balance with acidity, spice, umami, and the other elements of taste makes for the most delicious dishes. Within each recipe, the ingredients that directly contribute each of these tastes are annotated. We believe this will help you understand what each ingredient brings to a dish and therefore encourage you to experiment. For example, if a recipe calls for soy sauce (SALT, UMAMI) but last night's takeout sushi bender left your bottle empty, you know that you can deliver those same tastes to the recipe with any of the following: fish sauce, Worcestershire sauce, parmesan cheese, tomato paste, mushrooms, seaweed, or prosciutto.

Acidity in a dish can come in many forms as well. An ingredient list may show that acid is important in the recipe, but where that acid comes from is less so; lemon juice, lime juice, vinegar, and wine all contribute acidity to a dish, yet each with its own flavor. When it comes to the construction of a recipe, acidity is essential for the finished dish but the flavor that accompanies that acidity can be up to you. Basically, if you see a taste noted next to the ingredient, you know that you are free to swap that ingredient for another of your choice that provides the same taste. (Just remember to taste and adjust accordingly—vinegar and lime juice don't contribute the same level of acidity.) In the following chapter you will find a brief discussion of each of the tastes, what they typically contribute to a recipe, and the things you should keep in mind when substituting ingredients.

The thrust of this book, however, is its recipes—the elevated yet everyday dishes engineered for real life.

We've organized recipes the same way we eat—by dish or food group, not by meal. In our house, the only difference between lunch and dinner is the time of day it is consumed. And yes, cheese is its own food group in our house. We are equal opportunity eaters—eggs for dinner and steak for breakfast? If the mood strikes us, why not? We simply desire food that is interesting and delicious. You can mix and match dishes however you like.

Beyond that, you can also customize each recipe to perfectly suit your own—or your family's—tastes. Every recipe chapter begins with an introduction to the foods contained in that section. No matter what your skill level, these introductions are filled with information that will give you more confidence and competence in the kitchen. For instance, in the introduction to the chicken chapter you will learn the truth about cooking meat on the bone, why 165°F is an important temperature for chicken, and the best way to approach cooking different cuts of poultry. This information should also empower you to customize each recipe. Nearly all recipes can be easily adapted to be made with the cut of your choice—you might love grilled chicken breasts; others prefer chicken thighs when they fire up the coals.

Forno A Legna
From the Wood-Fired Oven

Verdure | Vegetables

Espresso Roasted Carrots

Pizza

Angeline's Pizza

Salty Cob

Piccoli Piatti

Wood Fired Meatballs

Dessert

SASSICAIA
BOLGHERI
ITALIA   2016

As you skim the recipes in the following pages, you will see how we devised each dish. It's the same way that James approaches the menu in our restaurant, Angelena's, in Pensacola, Florida. Each recipe begins with "ingredient inspirations," an interesting combination of ingredients that *The Flavor Matrix* suggested will taste great in a dish. In case you need a little more insight, we also share the specific chemical compound that contributes to that pairing and list the aromas the compound exhibits in the ingredients. We give that information for two reasons: First, to show how our previous research lead to the creation of this specific recipe. Second, and more important, we think this makes the creative part of cooking more transparent and will hopefully inspire further creations and variations on what we have begun here.

Once our ingredient inspiration was determined, we would write down those three to five ingredients on a notepad and treat them like a low-pressure mystery basket on an episode of *Chopped.* Sometimes the idea for the dish would come to us instantly; other times a combo rolled around the back of our heads for days or weeks. We would study the ingredients and think about them—what form could this ingredient take? Say, for example, we found eggs were a good pairing with another ingredient. Should we use boiled eggs? Maybe a hollandaise would be better? A super-eggy aioli might be easier to make. Cured egg yolks could be grated over the dish at the last minute. The possibilities for each ingredient were many and

varied. We chose one solution to the puzzle of those ingredients. It doesn't mean it was only way to put the pieces together, just the one that we liked best. Each set of ingredients might inspire you in a slightly different way. That's okay. Think of this book as a conversation, not a monologue.

With all of that said, if you're like us many days of the week and you need to just turn your brain off and cook because it's time for dinner, you can do that, too. We created these recipes to be accessible and approachable. Well suited for Wednesday dinner, with flavors that also fit at a holiday table.

Ingredients

FLAVOR PAIRING, IN 500 WORDS OR LESS

Our previous book, *The Flavor Matrix,* was developed around and dedicated to the art of flavor pairing. A relatively new concept in the culinary world, flavor pairing begins with understanding where the flavors in food come from. It's a process that requires examining food on a molecular level. But don't worry, there's no need to dust off a microscope before you get into the kitchen. You simply need to know that there are thousands of different chemical compounds naturally present in all foods, and each of those compounds has its own unique aroma. The combination of all these aromatic compounds in a single bite is what we call flavor. What you taste when you bite into an apple is the result of more than 400 different compounds all working together to create the unique flavor of that specific apple. Not to mention the sugars, acids, and textures that all contribute the perception of flavor—but more on that in a bit. Aromas in food can be wildly varied and often unexpected. Mesifurane, one of the most prominent aromas of fresh strawberries, actually smells like fresh-baked bread. Throughout this book you may see aromas that don't seem to fit with the food they are found in. Others may even seem unappetizing, like the compound toluene found in tomatoes, squash, and cheese, which is reminiscent of glue, paint, and solvent. However, its taste is nothing to turn your nose up at.

Understanding that these compounds create the flavor of each ingredient is step one in flavor pairing. In *The Flavor Matrix* we did a deep-dive breakdown of fifty-eight different ingredient groupings to illustrate how flavor is constructed in food. With that under our belts, we turned to the flavor pairing theory, a concept set forth by Heston Blumenthal and his R&D team at The Fat Duck. The flavor pairing theory states that if two ingredients share a significant number of flavor compounds, or if they have a single similar compound in high concentration, then we can predict that those two ingredients will taste good when combined in a dish. Every recipe we share in this book is based on this idea that the ingredients are chemically matched for maximum deliciousness.

Well-matched flavors are essential in any great dish, but taste cannot be left as an afterthought. The most perfectly matched flavors will fall flat if not accompanied by dynamic and balanced tastes. What's the difference? Flavors come from aromatic compounds that are detected by the nose. Taste comes from elements of food that are detected by the tongue. There are currently six tastes that we are aware of: fat, sour, salt, umami, bitter, and sweet. Each of these is recognized by dedicated receptors on the tongue. Other qualities like spicy and astringent are also detected in the mouth, but by a different mechanism than the six *tastes* listed above. To be a great cook, it is important to understand what each of these elements does in food, both in the structure of a recipe and its sensory qualities in a finished dish.

FAT

Fat, an essential nutrient, has only recently been recognized as a taste. It was always known to contribute to mouthfeel, the physical sensation created in the mouth by a bite of food, but in the past few years scientists have discovered that there are cells on the tongue that respond to the presence of free fatty acids in food. Fat enhances the tastes of umami, sweet, and salty and balances the taste of spiciness in food.

In most recipes, fat is relied on to coat foods, prevent sticking, promote browning, and/or provide moisture. Any fat can accomplish these; however, the type of fat you choose will have an effect on the final flavor of the dish. The best way to demonstrate this is with scrambled eggs. Imagine you make three batches of scrambled eggs, one with butter, one with olive oil, and one with sesame oil. They will all cook the same and the finished product of all three will look identical. However, the flavor of each egg will be dramatically different. Eggs have very little flavor on their own, so the flavors of the different fats will really come through. When used properly, no one fat is better than another; it is simply a matter of preference.

In something simple like a scrambled egg, the type of fat used has little impact on the finished dish beyond the flavor. If, instead of eggs, you were sautéing a chicken breast, you would need to consider not only the flavor of the fat you wanted to use, but also how it holds up at a high temperature. This quality of fats, known

as the smoke point, is the temperature at which a fat begins to break down. When a fat reaches its smoke point, it will begin to impart off flavors to the food and cause the food to brown or burn more quickly. Foods will not begin to brown in a sauté pan or on a grill until their surface temperature surpasses 300°F, and the external temperature should actually be at least 350°F to create browning without completely drying out the food. As you will see from the chart below, whole butter, extra-virgin olive oil, coconut oil, and sesame oil break down at those temperatures, so they should not be the primary fat used for browning meats. You will also note that this chart dispels the common cooking myth that you should never fry in olive oil. Frying in olive oil is fine, and is done commonly throughout Italy. What you should consider, however, is that the olive oil will impart a specific flavor into the food while frying. Also, olive oil is not nearly as durable as other oils, so it will need to be replaced more often if frying large quantities, which gets expensive. A final word about olive oil: the compounds that give extra-virgin olive oils their unique flavors will break down even before the oil reaches its smoke point. This means that expensive oils with deep, complex flavors should never be heated. They should be reserved for finishing and dressing items just before serving.

Whole butter is more than just fat. Most butters are around 80 percent fat, the other 20 percent a combination of water and milk solids. Milk solids contribute a significant amount of flavor, but they are delicate and will burn well before the fat in

TYPE OF FAT	SMOKE POINT
Safflower oil	510°F
Light or refined olive oil	465°F
Soybean oil	450°F
Peanut oil	450°F
Clarified butter or ghee	450°F
Corn oil	450°F
Sunflower oil	440°F
Vegetable oil	400–450°F
Canola oil	400°F
Grapeseed oil	390°F
Lard	370°F
Vegetable shortening	360°F
Sesame oil	350–410°F
Butter	350°F
Coconut oil	350°F
Extra-virgin olive oil	325–375°F

the butter reaches the smoke point. This is why melted whole butter and clarified butter/ghee (from which the milk solids have been removed) have different smoke points. Whole butter works well to promote browning of other foods, but it can burn at high temperatures so it is not ideal for searing. In baking, fats are not as easily swapped for one another. Because of its unique composition, butter can provide structure in baked goods that oil does not. In nonbaking recipes you can use any type of oil you'd like, as long as the temperature capacity is appropriate. Just remember that the oil you choose will affect the flavor of your finished dish.

ACID/SOUR

Acid's main job in a recipe is to punctuate (provide a little punch) and help balance other tastes. Specifically, acid is the counter to sweet and fat, though it works with these tastes in different ways. Sour is the taste opposite of sweet, so adding acidity to a dish will effectively reduce the amount of sweetness perceived in a dish. Fat can overwhelm the palate, coating the tongue and making the all other tastes more difficult to perceive. Acidity in a dish will help cut through that fat, in a sense cleaning the palate and preparing it receive new tastes.

Acid can also work to *denature* proteins, as in ceviche. (Denaturation is the more accurate name for what happens to a protein in both the cooking and curing processes.) Acid essentially "cooks" the protein. This is why marinades that include vinegar or citrus juice (specifically lemon or lime) should only be used for short periods; otherwise the acid in the marinade will begin to "cook" the protein before your ever get it on the grill, which can leave the meat dry or tough.

Acid can have a similar effect on plant cells, breaking down the cell walls and collapsing the structure of the plant. This is the wilted-salad effect. If combining an acid with crisp raw fruits or vegetables, it should be done at the last minute to preserve the texture. Leafy salads should tossed with dressing just moments before serving, while coleslaw is best dressed well in advance so the crunchy cabbage can soften. Acid also breaks down chlorophyll in green vegetables, causing them to turn from vibrant green to a dull olive-green. This effect is amplified under heat, so if you want your sautéed green beans to taste bright and lemony, you should add only lemon zest while they cook and give them light squeeze of fresh lemon juice after they are on the plate.

SALT

Salt works to enhance the perception of all other tastes. Salt is like an alarm clock for taste buds; it makes sure they are on their toes and ready to grab whatever tastes are coming. In low concentrations, salt will suppress the perception of bitter tastes, effectively making foods taste sweeter. This is why a small amount of salt is essential in any sweet dish. In higher concentrations typical of savory dishes, salt enhances the perception of umami. Salt also helps to draw moisture out of food, as it does in the curing process. However, you don't need to be curing foods for this quality to greatly enhance a dish. Lightly salting meat before cook-ing it can help remove moisture from the surface, allowing it to develop a better sear when cooked. It can also draw excess moisture from proteins, fruits, or vegeta-bles to help concentrate their flavor.

While salt helps to draw moisture out of food, it can also help proteins retain mois-ture when cooked (read: be juicier). When salt is dissolved into water, as in a brine, muscle fibers in proteins will absorb the excess moisture through the process of osmosis in an effort to reach equilibrium. When the proteins in the muscle denature in cooking, that moisture is retained in a matrix created by the unraveling pro-teins—and your meat is juicier.

When you salt your food matters. Salt should be added gradually throughout the cooking process. This will help all components of the recipe to be properly seasoned. The best illustration of this is cooking rice: Boil one cup of rice in salted water so that the rice absorbs salt throughout the cooking process. Boil a second cup of rice with no salt and stir the salt into the rice once it is finished cooking. The difference in the taste of the two will be dramatic. The rice cooked in salted water will have a more rounded, fuller flavor, because the salt has been completely absorbed during the cooking process and slowly releases to the tongue. The rice salted after cooking will taste salty because the salt remains on the surface of the grains, hitting the tongue immediately and overwhelming salt sensors. Yet as you chew the grains of rice they will taste flat and bland.

UMAMI

Umami is that what-makes-this-taste-so-good element in food that can sometimes be hard to identify. Umami was recognized as a taste in 1908 by a researcher at Tokyo University, but it did not gain wide recogni-tion or acceptance until nearly 100 years later. Umami is sometimes described as savoriness, and is identified on the tongue by detection of glutamate, an amino acid. Umami cannot be created in the cooking process in the same way that sweetness can be developed by slowly caramelizing onions; rather it is naturally present in ingredients. However, umami can develop over time and is found in all fermented and aged ingredients. Think of umami as

Umami-Rich Foods

Seaweed

Tomatoes

Garlic

Asparagus

Mushrooms

Truffles

Scallops

Shrimp

Uni

Clams

Mussels

Anchovies

Cured hams

Parmesan cheese

Miso

Soy sauce

Fish sauce

Oyster sauce

Kimchi

Eggs

a flavor secret weapon. Anytime you can add umami-containing ingredients to a recipe—savory or sweet—it will help to enhance all other tastes.

BITTER

Foods that are overly bitter are generally not palatable. However, bitterness in food can be desirable when properly crafted. Bitterness in food generally comes from tannins, naturally occurring phenolic compounds found in a variety of ingredients like coffee, tea, plants in the Brassicaceae family (such as broccoli and Brussels sprouts), olives, some nuts, and cocoa. Bitterness is a smaller but important part of the taste puzzle and should not be ignored in recipes. Without the pleasant bitterness of cocoa, a pan of brownies would be more like a big block of sugar cookie.

Bitter is also believed to have some psychological effects on appetite. In many cultures a sip of something bitter—Campari, Pernod, or ouzo—is consumed before a meal to help stimulate the appetite. Research has shown that bitter compounds do, in fact, stimulate the release of hunger hormones. Bitter foods can also stimulate the production of saliva and stomach acid, aiding the digestion process.

SWEET

The human body is programmed to crave sweet foods. They are instantly recognized as a good source of quick energy. In food, sweet plays well with all other tastes: enhancing salty, umami, and fat, and balancing sour and bitter. While sweet tends to be the dominant taste in desserts, it remains an important component of savory recipes as well. As with all other tastes, the goal with sweet should be to create balance. Rarely when constructing a recipe do you want to allow one taste to dominate, in the same way that a symphony dominated by brass instruments won't sound as pleasing.

When looking to build flavor in a dish, we prefer to find ways of developing sweetness that go beyond simply adding sugar. Sweeteners come in many forms and sugars are naturally present in most fruits and vegetables. Careful cooking can enhance the natural sugars in most foods. There are also ingredients that enhance the perception of sweetness. Citrus zest, vanilla, and warm spices such as cinnamon, nutmeg, and allspice can all make foods taste sweeter without adding sugar in any form.

VEGETABLES

Vegetables

Preparing vegetables and fruits can be a tricky undertaking. Taste and texture are extremely important. Think of that perfectly ripe summer strawberry, still warm from the sun. You bite into it, it's juicy and sweet with just a touch of acidity. The creamy flesh yields to tiny, crunchy seeds as its perfect perfume fills your nose. For those few, fleeting weeks when strawberries are at their peak, nothing could be better. But for the rest of the year strawberries just aren't the same—too firm, too much acidity, too soft, no aroma—any number of shortcomings leave you underwhelmed. There is no way to replicate what nature does so perfectly, but we can get close—adding a few drops of vinegar to overly sweet strawberries, a pinch of sugar to ones that are too tart. With a little time, that sugar will also help soften their texture, though if left to marinate too long, they turn to mush. If you learn to think of each ingredient as its individual components of taste, you will understand how to best prepare it. In this chapter, we try to find ways to get the absolute best out of each ingredient, whether it's carefully assembling a salad dressing to fully complement the green aromas of lettuces or coaxing a sweet, smokiness from the simple leek.

One of the most common questions we get from home cooks is: "Why do vegetables at restaurants taste so much better than the vegetables I cook at home?"

The answer is simple: the majority of people overcook and underseason vegetables. Couple that with the fact that restaurants are buying their vegetables from the same people that sell to your local grocery store, meaning restaurants are typically serving you vegetables that are days—if not weeks—fresher than when you purchase them from a grocery store and prepare them yourself. So how do you get better vegetables at home?

SO HOW DO YOU GET BETTER VEGETABLES AT HOME?

1

Cook your vegetables less.

2

Season them more—that means salt, spices, and other aromatic ingredients.

3

Shop at a farmers' market or learn how to pick out the freshest vegetables at your local grocery store.

COOK VEGETABLES LESS

Texture is one of the most overlooked factors in taste. Research has shown that crispy textures greatly enhance the perception of freshness in food as well as enjoyment. An Oxford University study that had participants wear headphones while eating from the same bowl of potato chips found that those with loud crunching noises playing in their headphones perceived the potato chips as fresher and more flavorful than those with muffled sounds playing in theirs.

When vegetables are fresh and properly prepared, they should retain some of their natural crunch, making them taste better. This chapter will explore a number of different methods for preparing vegetables. Many involve cooking, some will not. Heat, salt, and acid are the main methods of softening a vegetable's texture. This is extremely important to keep in mind in the kitchen. If you want crisp greens and a lively crunch in your salad, you should not season or dress it until just moments before serving. On the other hand, if you find yourself with tomatoes that are a bit bland and mealy, dress them with vinegar and salt early on to help soften their texture and enhance their flavor.

When it comes to cooking, the best method varies depending on the item, but high heat and short cooking times are generally best for most vegetables. Cooking vegetables quickly with high heat allows you to soften and flavor the exterior while maintaining the texture of the interior.

SEASON MORE

Salt matters. Salt's role in food in food is to enhance flavor. Though we refer to it as "seasoning," salt is a flavor enhancer. It is not adding flavor to your food, just giving more oomph to the flavors that are already there. It does this in two ways: First, by drawing water out of foods, thereby concentrating their natural flavor. And second, salt acts directly on your tongue, waking up your taste buds. Our bodies naturally crave salt, because it is essential for normal function in our cells. Crunch and salt are the reason we love snack foods so much—it's programmed into our brains.

However, salt is only one part of the seasoning equation. The dishes we all love to eat have their salty elements but also provide complex flavors through aromas found in herbs and spices, match sweetness with bracing acidity, and punctuate with heat or spiciness. When creating a new recipe for our restaurant or cooking at home every day, we try to look at how many different elements of taste—salt, sweet, sour, spicy, bitter, umami, and fat—we can incorporate through creative (but not complex) seasoning.

SEEK FRESHNESS

It's quite simple: Fresh food tastes better. The moment a fruit or vegetable is picked from its plant, it begins to change. Green peas, for example, immediately begin to convert their sugar into starch to preserve their energy source, meaning that peas quickly transform from tender and sweet to firm and starchy. This is why frozen green peas are often the best option, since they are frozen immediately after harvest, at their peak of freshness. Other vegetables are harvested anticipating the changes they will undergo. Tomatoes are often picked in their underripe, green state so that they can survive the days- or sometimes weeks-long journey to your grocery store shelves and ultimately your kitchen.

Fruits and vegetables that are allowed to fully ripen on the plant have more time to develop taste and flavor from their environment. The items must then be transported to market and consumed more quickly. However, there are some fruits that will continue to ripen and improve in taste after they are harvested. These include apricots, avocados, bananas, cantaloupes, kiwi, mangoes, nectarines, peaches, pears, plantains, plums, and tomatoes. Produce that does not improve, but should picked only when ripe, includes apples, cherries, corn, cucumbers, eggplant, grapefruit, grapes, oranges, pineapple, strawberries, tangerines, watermelon, zucchini, and squash. When selecting vegetables, look for items that are firm to the touch, show little sign of scars or bruising, and have smooth, tight skin. Don't be afraid of irregularly-shaped—or "ugly"—fruits and vegetables; they are just as flavorful.

When storing fruits and vegetables, the general rule is that the refrigerator should be used for preservation—to either slow the ripening process or extend the ripe state. Tomatoes are a great example. They should be stored at room temperature until they are fully ripe. Once ripened, if you're not ready to eat them, you can move them to the refrigerator to extend their shelf life by three days (or more). That said, refrigerating tomatoes isn't ideal. If you've ever felt like refrigerated tomatoes don't quite taste the same—you're right! Some of the compounds responsible for a tomato's aroma will be destroyed at temperatures below 55°F. Other produce sensitive to refrigeration include stone fruits (such as peaches, plums, apricots), melons, avocadoes, and citrus.

Asparagus is also best kept at room temperature. When you get asparagus home, trim a thin slice from the base of the stalks, then stand them up in a jar of water as you would for fresh flowers. This will prevent the delicate tips of the asparagus from collecting water and going bad. Most other green vegetables are sensitive to excess moisture as well. They should never be stored in closed plastic bags or sealed containers, which trap the moisture that plants release and cause the plants to break down ("go bad") more quickly. A bowl with dampened paper towels (to preserve moisture) draped over the top or another breathable container is the ideal storage container for lettuces, kale, spinach, or herbs.

UMAMI IN A BOTTLE

lettuce, mustard, fennel, vinegar

This is our ultimate salad dressing. We selected each of the ingredients for its chemical affinity for the others and because each pairs extraordinarily well with the green aromas found in leafy greens.

MAKES about
1 cup dressing

COMPOUND
tridecane

AROMA
bay leaf, allspice,
lemon balm

3 cloves garlic, minced or finely grated UMAMI

1 tablespoon Dijon mustard
SPICY, ACID

1 tablespoon soy sauce or fish sauce SALT, UMAMI

½ teaspoon ground fennel seeds

¼ cup red wine vinegar SOUR

½ cup olive oil FAT

Combine the garlic, mustard, soy sauce, fennel seeds, and vinegar in a small jar or bottle. Place the lid on and shake vigorously to mix. Add the olive oil and mix again. Adjust the seasoning to taste—adding more soy sauce if salt is needed or more mustard for spice—and balance the oil and vinegar to taste. Store in the refrigerator for up to 4 weeks. Shake vigorously before using.

The standard ratio for salad dressings is 3 parts oil to 1 part vinegar. Here, we've reduced the amount of oil for a little more "punch." But if you find the dressing too tart, add more oil to taste.

―――

When tasting your dressing, dip a leaf of lettuce, a carrot stick, or other vegetable into the mixed dressing. This will give you a more accurate representation of what your salad will taste like. Dressings will always seem too strong if you taste them directly from a spoon.

COCO-SLAW

coconut milk, cabbage, cilantro, carrot

Coleslaw with a tropical twist. Coconut and cabbage are an unexpected and delicious combination. The thing we love about this recipe (besides how good it is) is that it makes a rich, creamy slaw that is cookout approved—no mayo to sit in the sun and get funky. You could also omit the cabbage and make just the dressing. It's a delicious vegan dressing that pairs nicely with all dark leafy greens, such as kale. Serve this slaw with fish tacos, grilled or roasted pork, or grilled or roasted pineapple.

SERVES 8

COMPOUND
1-tetradecanol

AROMA
coconut

1 head green cabbage, shredded (about 12 cups)

2 teaspoons kosher salt SALT

1 teaspoon chili powder SPICY

One 14-ounce can coconut milk FAT

2 cups shredded carrots (about 3 medium carrots) SWEET

1 jalapeño chile, diced SPICY

¼ cup roughly chopped fresh cilantro

Juice of 2 limes SOUR

Use chili powder (the spice blend) instead of a pure ground chile like ancho because it adds a touch of cumin, which really complements the other ingredients.

———

It is worth it to grate the carrots fresh so that some of the carrot juice makes it into the dressing.

Place the cabbage in a large bowl. Add the salt and chili powder and mix well. Continue mixing and tightly squeezing handfuls of the cabbage for 1 minute, to help the salt penetrate and soften the cabbage. Transfer the cabbage to a colander in the sink and wipe the bowl dry.

In the dry bowl, combine the coconut milk, carrot, jalapeño, cilantro, and lime juice. Mix well. Add the drained cabbage to the bowl and toss to combine. Cover and refrigerate until you're ready to serve, up to 3 days.

GRILLED LEEKS VINAIGRETTE

allium, mushrooms, almonds, feta, tarragon

This is our fresh take on the classic French dish leeks vinaigrette. When alliums of any variety (anything in the onion/garlic family) are cooked, their pungent sulphur compounds diminish and they become sweet. At the same time, charring or cooking over open flame adds smoky depth. Sour flavors are a natural pairing to the earthiness of leeks and mushrooms. Yet the strongest affinity in the recipe is the combination of mushrooms, tarragon, and allium.

SERVES 4

COMPOUND
1-octen-3-one

AROMAS
earth, metal, mushroom

¼ **cup white wine vinegar** SOUR

2 **cloves garlic, finely grated**
UMAMI

1 **tablespoon minced fresh tarragon, plus more for garnish**

3 **medium leeks**

3 **portabella mushroom caps, wiped clean, gills removed**
UMAMI

1 **teaspoon kosher salt, plus more as needed** SALT

¼ **cup extra-virgin olive oil** FAT

2 **tablespoons good-quality balsamic vinegar** SOUR, SWEET

In a small bowl, combine the white wine vinegar, garlic, and tarragon. Mix well and set aside for the flavors to develop.

To prepare the leeks, trim away the dark green leafy portion (the light green is okay). There is a natural separation where the leek turns from solid and onion-like to dark green and looser; this is where you want to cut. Discard the dark green portion or reserve for making stocks or soups.

Do not trim the root end of the leek—this will help it hold together during cooking. Split the leeks in half lengthwise, cutting through the root. Rinse the leeks thoroughly, pulling back the layers under running water to wash away any trapped dirt or sand. Pat the leeks dry and place them in a 13 x 9-inch baking dish along with the mushrooms. Pour the vinegar mixture over the vegetables and turn them to coat well. Sprinkle with salt and drizzle with the olive oil. Leave at room temperature to marinate while you heat the grill, or cover and refrigerate for up to 36 hours before cooking.

The reason for the difference in color in the two parts of the leek is chlorophyll. The parts of the plant that grow above ground are exposed to the sun and therefore are able to develop chlorophyll. The dark green top has spent a lot of time above ground, the pale green middle recently reached above the soil and has developed a little chlorophyll, and the white stalk remained underground through the leek's life span.

The marinade will not only flavor the leeks before they cook, but will also help soften both the texture of the leeks and their strong allium aroma.

¼ cup sliced almonds, toasted FAT

½ cup feta cheese crumbles
FAT, SALT, SOUR, UMAMI

Your oven is the best place to toast nuts: Preheat it to 325°F and spread the nuts in a single layer on a baking sheet. Toast in the oven until golden and aromatic, 4 to 6 minutes, depending on size.

Heat a grill to medium.

Place the leeks and mushrooms, cut side down, on the hot grill, with the leeks at a 45-degree angle to the grates. Set aside the baking dish with the marinade. Cook the vegetables undisturbed for 3 to 4 minutes, then rotate each piece 90 degrees. Cook for another 3 to 4 minutes, then flip and repeat the process on the second side. At this point the mushrooms should be tender all the way through and be pierced easily with the tip of knife. Return the mushrooms to the dish with the marinade.

Depending on the size of the leeks, they may need to cook for 4 to 8 minutes more. The leeks should be tender all the way through and well charred on the edges. When they are done, return them to the dish with the mushrooms and turn to coat well with the remaining marinade.

To serve, slice the leeks crosswise into 2-inch sections, discarding the root. Cut the mushroom caps in half, then cut the halves into slices approximately ½ inch thick. Return the cut vegetables to the dish with the marinade one more time and gently toss to coat. Season to taste with salt. Arrange the dressed vegetables on a platter and drizzle with the balsamic vinegar. Top with the almonds, feta, and more tarragon.

AVOCADO TOAST

avocado, fennel, apple, cocoa, ancho chile

Avocado and fennel are great match; so are fennel and apple. Think we're joking? Try a little minced apple and fennel in your guacamole some time. But the best pairings for avocado are deep, earthy flavors like cocoa and chile.

SERVES 4

COMPOUND
linalool

AROMAS
bergamot, citrus, coriander, floral, lavender, lemon, rose

¹/₈ teaspoon ancho chile powder or other dark chile powder SPICY

¹/₈ teaspoon unsweetened cocoa powder BITTER

1 teaspoon kosher salt SALT

1 teaspoon fennel seeds

2 avocadoes FAT

Juice of ¹/₂ lime SOUR

¹/₄ cup diced apple SWEET

4 slices rustic sourdough or 7-grain bread UMAMI

2 tablespoons extra-virgin olive oil FAT

1 clove garlic, halved UMAMI

You want a mildly sweet and crunchy apple like Honeycrisp or Braeburn.

In a small dish, combine the chile powder, cocoa, and salt. Mix well and reserve for garnish.

Heat a cast-iron pan or heavy-bottomed skillet over medium heat. When hot, add the fennel seeds. Swirl the pan until the seeds become very fragrant, no more than 30 seconds, then immediately transfer them to a cutting board so they do not burn. Press the seeds with the back of a large spoon or the side of knife to crush and break them into smaller pieces. Turn the heat off and leave the pan on the stove.

Cut the avocadoes in half and remove the pits. Scoop the flesh from the skin and cut into 1-inch chunks. Place the avocado pieces in a bowl and add the fennel seeds, lime juice, and apple. Mix well.

Turn the heat back to medium on the pan. Lightly coat the slices of bread with the olive oil and toast in the hot pan until golden brown and slightly dark at the edges, 45 to 60 seconds per side. Work in batches if necessary. When all the bread is toasted, remove the skillet from the heat and rub one side of the bread with the cut garlic. Set the toasts aside.

Divide the avocado mixture evenly between the pieces of toast and gently press to spread it over the surface. Sprinkle each toast with the salt mixture and serve immediately.

Toasting in a skillet is the ideal method for bread that is toasted and crisp on the exterior with a soft, chewy interior—aka perfect toast.

AVOCADO "SUCCOTASH"

avocado, corn, tomato, basil

Our succotash—really, our kids' favorite version of a Mexican salsa—balances a variety of tastes, textures, and different notes within one flavor category: All of the ingredients have strong fruit-like/vegetal aromas that make them an ideal match. It's beautiful in its simplicity and as delicious served with tortilla chips as it is atop grilled white fish or chicken.

SERVES 4

COMPOUND
ethyl acetate

AROMAS
brandy, contact glue, grape, sweet

3 tablespoons extra-virgin olive oil, plus more as needed FAT

3 ears fresh yellow corn, shucked SWEET

Kosher salt SALT

Freshly ground black pepper SPICY

1 avocado, pitted, peeled, and diced FAT

1 cup diced fresh tomato ACID, UMAMI

2 tablespoons chopped fresh basil

Grated zest and juice of ½ lime SOUR

¼ teaspoon Basque pepper powder (piment d'espelette), cayenne pepper, or red pepper flakes SPICY

Heat a grill to hot and oil the grates, or preheat the broiler. Lightly drizzle the corn with olive oil. Rub the oil over the corn to distribute it, then season the corn well with salt and black pepper. If using the broiler, set the corn on a baking sheet. Grill or broil the corn, turning frequently, until the kernels are brown and toasted, 6 to 8 minutes. Let cool until cool enough to handle, then shave the kernels off the cob with a sharp chef's knife (see tip, page 102).

In a large bowl, combine the corn kernels, avocado, tomato, basil, lime zest and juice, Basque pepper, and 3 tablespoons olive oil. Season with salt and pepper to taste and serve immediately.

Take your time to properly char the corn. As the kernels blacken, they will become smoky and sweet. Don't worry, they will not get tough or bitter. You want to burn them.

ROASTED BEET SALAD

beet, orange, mint, hazelnuts, yogurt

Beets and orange are a phenomenal pairing. In *The Flavor Matrix,* we scored them as a nearly 60 percent match, which is exceptional. Beets become very sweet when roasted, so when pairing them with orange, you need plenty of acidity. In this recipe we get that from vinegar, lemon, and yogurt. Both parts of this dish—the roasted beets and the yogurt dressing—can be made in advance and combined just before serving.

SERVES 4 to 6

COMPOUND
2-isopropyl-3-methoxypyrazine

AROMAS
bell pepper, earth, green, hazelnut, pea

2 pounds beets UMAMI

2 tablespoons olive oil FAT

1 tablespoon kosher salt SALT

½ teaspoon freshly ground black pepper SPICY

4 branches fresh thyme

1 bay leaf (optional)

½ cup white wine vinegar SOUR

Zest of 1 orange, removed in strips with a vegetable peeler SWEET

1 cup plain Greek yogurt FAT, SOUR, UMAMI

Grated zest and juice of 1 lemon SOUR

2 tablespoons chopped fresh mint, plus a few small leaves for garnish

½ teaspoon ground coriander

Pinch cayenne pepper

½ cup toasted hazelnuts (see tip, page 21) FAT

Preheat the oven to 350°F.

Trim and rinse the beets. Toss them with the olive oil, salt, and black pepper. Place the beets in small baking dish or pan just large enough to hold them in a single layer. Add the thyme, bay leaf (if using), and vinegar. Cover with aluminum foil and roast until tender, 25 minutes for baby beets, 40 minutes for medium beets, and up to 75 minutes for larger ones. You should be able to easily pierce the beets all the way through with the tip of a knife.

Let cool slightly, until just cool enough to handle. Use a paper towel or kitchen towel to wipe the skins from the beets.

Cut each beet into bite-size pieces. Place the beets in a bowl and pour over some of the juices from the roasting pan. Toss to coat, and season to taste with salt and pepper. Add the orange zest and mix again. If not serving immediately, refrigerate in a covered container for up to 10 days.

In a separate bowl, combine the yogurt, lemon zest and juice, chopped mint, coriander, and cayenne. Mix well. If not serving immediately, refrigerate in a covered container for up to 3 days.

To serve, spread the dressing over a large platter. Mound the beets over the dressing. Garnish with the hazelnuts and mint leaves.

Peel the beets as soon as they are cool enough to handle, holding them with a towel. The skins can be easily rubbed away at this point. As the beets cool, the skins will become much more difficult to remove.

Adding the zest to the beets after roasting means it will keep its bright, fresh aroma.

A DIFFERENT KIND OF GREEN SALAD

cucumber, melon, jalapeño

This one might sound a little crazy but hexanal—a chemical compound that smells like freshly-cut grass—is responsible for how well these seemingly disparate ingredients come together in this big, beautiful salad. Plus, this is textbook taste development—you get sweet, salty, savory, spicy, and fresh all in one amazing package.

SERVES 4
as a side

COMPOUND
hexanal

AROMAS
fresh, fruit, grass, green, oil

2 cups thinly sliced Kirby cucumbers (3 or 4 cucumbers)

1 cup halved seedless green grapes SWEET

2 cups cubed honeydew melon SWEET

½ green jalapeño chile, thinly sliced SPICY

Grated zest and juice of 1 lime SOUR

1 cup coarsely chopped baby arugula BITTER, SPICY

2 teaspoons kosher salt SALT

½ teaspoon freshly ground black pepper SPICY

¼ cup extra-virgin olive oil FAT

1 teaspoon toasted fennel seeds

Shaved parmesan cheese, for garnish SALT, UMAMI

In a large bowl, combine the cucumbers, grapes, melon, jalapeño, lime zest and juice, and arugula. Season with salt and pepper and toss well to combine. Transfer to a large platter or serving bowl. Refrigerate until you're ready to serve.

Just before serving, drizzle the salad with olive oil, then sprinkle with the fennel seeds and parmesan shavings.

This can be done up to 4 hours in advance. If left for too long, the acid in the lime juice will start to make the fruits mushy. If you need to prepare everything in advance, mix the jalapeño, lime, salt, pepper, and olive oil in a bowl, but keep them separate from the fruits and arugula and mix just before serving.

WATERMELON BRUSCHETTA

watermelon, tomato, pecorino

The beauty of this dish is the visual trick it plays: when mixed together, the cubes of watermelon and tomato are nearly indiscernible, while they alternate savory and sweet bursts on the palate. You're probably not thinking garlic, basil, and cheese with your watermelon, but trust us on this one.

SERVES 4

COMPOUND
1-penten-3-one

AROMAS
green, herb, mustard, pungent

2 cups finely diced seedless watermelon SWEET

1 cup diced fresh tomato UMAMI

½ teaspoon fine sea salt SALT

4 slices rustic sourdough bread UMAMI

¼ cup extra-virgin olive oil FAT

2 cloves garlic, peeled UMAMI

1 tablespoon chopped fresh basil

Freshly ground black pepper, for garnish

Shaved pecorino cheese, for garnish SALT, UMAMI

Combine the watermelon and tomato in a bowl and add the salt. Gently mix to combine, then transfer to a colander in the sink and leave to drain for 10 to 20 minutes.

Brush the slices of sourdough with about half of the olive oil. Toast on both sides in a skillet or on a grill until lightly charred on the edges. Rub the toasted bread with the garlic on one side and set aside.

Transfer the drained watermelon and tomato to a clean bowl. Add the remaining olive oil and the basil. Gently toss to combine. Spoon the watermelon mixture onto the toasted bread and garnish with pepper and a generous shaving of pecorino.

The tomatoes and watermelon will expel a good deal of excess water at this point, helping to intensify their flavors.

SICILIAN-STYLE PEACH SALAD

peach, fennel, olives, mint, chile

This salad celebrates the two places we love most—the American South and coastal Italy. This recipe is based on a classic Sicilian salad made with oranges, but substitutes the quintessential Southern peach. Try to select firm peaches that are slightly underripe. They add great crunch and a touch of tartness.

SERVES 4 to 6

COMPOUND
alpha-phellandrene

AROMAS
citrus, mint, pepper, turpentine, wood

3 tablespoons white wine vinegar SOUR

1 teaspoon honey SWEET

½ teaspoon kosher salt, plus more as needed SALT

½ jalapeño chile, sliced SPICY

¼ cup thinly sliced red onion

2 firm peaches, pitted and sliced SWEET

1 head fennel, thinly sliced

½ cup pitted and halved Castelvetrano green olives SALT, UMAMI

2 tablespoons chopped fresh mint, plus whole leaves for garnish

¼ cup extra-virgin olive oil FAT

¼ cup crumbled or grated salty cheese (such as feta or pecorino; optional) FAT, SALT, UMAMI

Combine the vinegar, honey, and salt in small bowl. Mix well until dissolved. Add the jalapeño and onion and set aside to marinate while you prepare the salad.

In a large bowl, combine the peaches, fennel, olives, and mint. Add the olive oil and season lightly with salt. Gently toss to combine. Add the vinegar mixture and toss gently. Transfer to a platter and garnish with extra mint leaves and cheese, if desired.

Slicing the onion, peaches, and fennel on a mandoline will yield the best results.

The vinegar will pull some of the heat (capsaicin) from the chile and distribute it more evenly throughout the salad, while also mellowing the pungency of the onions.

—

Adding the vinegar after everything is coated with oil will slow the softening, keeping the peach and fennel from becoming mushy after mixing.

BRUSSELS SPROUTS KEBABS

brussels sprouts, chipotle chile, yogurt, dill

Brussels sprouts are unbelievably delicious when charred on a grill. The only problem is that because of their size, they're really hard to cook that way. So we decided to line them up on skewers so they could be cooked easily, with a pair of grill tongs in one hand and a drink in the other. Brussels sprouts pair really well with green and dairy flavors, making the accompanying yogurt-dill sauce perfect to dunk them in.

SERVES 4

COMPOUND
methyl octanoate

AROMAS
fruit, orange, sweet, wax, wine

SAUCE

1 clove garlic, peeled UMAMI

1 teaspoon chipotle-based hot sauce SPICY

1 tablespoon fresh lemon juice SOUR

½ cup plain Greek yogurt FAT, SOUR, UMAMI

1 tablespoon chopped fresh dill

BRUSSELS SPROUTS

18 Brussels sprouts UMAMI

½ teaspoon ground cumin

1 teaspoon garlic powder

2 teaspoons honey SWEET

2 tablespoons extra-virgin olive oil FAT

Kosher salt SALT

Instead of fresh dill, you can mix 1 teaspoon dried dill with 1 tablespoon fresh flat-leaf parsley leaves and chop the two together. This will give you the fresh green aromas that dry herbs typically lack and deliver distinctive dill aroma.

Make the sauce: Finely grate the garlic with a Microplane or use a garlic press. Combine the garlic, hot sauce, and lemon juice in a small bowl and stir well. Leave for 5 minutes for the flavors to develop. Add the yogurt and dill and mix well. Store, covered, in the refrigerator until you're ready to serve, up to 3 days.

Cook the Brussels sprouts: Bring a large pot of salted water to a boil. Trim the ends from the Brussels sprouts and cut each one in half. Drop the sprouts into the boiling water and cook for 1 minute. Remove the sprouts with a spider or slotted spoon and spread them in a single layer on a baking sheet to air-dry.

Meanwhile, heat a grill to hot and oil the grates.

In a large bowl, combine the cumin and garlic powder with 1 tablespoon hot tap water. Once the spices have absorbed the water and formed a thick paste, stir in the honey and olive oil.

Mixing the spices with water before using makes them more aromatic and flavorful.

When the Brussels sprouts are cool enough to handle but still a little warm, add them to the spice paste and toss well to coat. Arrange the Brussels sprout halves on skewers so the flat cut sides line up on each skewer. Season each skewer with kosher salt. Grill for 2 to 3 minutes on the first side, until the vegetables begin to lightly char, then flip and cook on the second side until tender through, another 2 to 3 minutes. Remove the skewers from the grill and arrange on a platter. Serve with the yogurt sauce.

If using wooden skewers, soak the skewers in room temperature water for at least 30 minutes, up to overnight to prevent them from burning when on the grill.

CAESAR ARTICHOKE DIP
artichoke, anchovy, lemon

This is party food taken to the next level: spinach-artichoke dip meets Caesar salad. The combination of artichoke, anchovy, and lemon is basically the beginning of every meal we've ever eaten in Rome. But here we bring it to a more playful and comfortable place. Let's face it—a creamy, cheesy dip is always a good idea.

SERVES 6

COMPOUND
heptanal

AROMAS
citrus, dry fish, fat, green, nut, rancid

2 large egg yolks FAT

3 flat anchovy fillets, rinsed and drained UMAMI

¼ teaspoon freshly ground black pepper SPICY

¼ teaspoon smoked paprika

Pinch of cayenne pepper SPICY

4 cloves garlic, peeled UMAMI

½ cup grated parmesan cheese FAT, SALT, UMAMI

1 tablespoon fresh lemon juice SOUR

1 tablespoon red wine vinegar SOUR

2 teaspoons Worcestershire sauce UMAMI

3 dashes Tabasco sauce SPICY

1 tablespoon Dijon mustard SPICY

4 ounces cream cheese, softened FAT

½ cup sour cream FAT, SOUR

One 15-ounce can quartered artichoke hearts in water

One 8- or 9-ounce bag or bunch spinach, chopped (about 4 cups)

Kosher salt SALT

½ baguette, thinly sliced

Extra-virgin olive oil, for brushing the baguette

Combine the egg yolks, anchovies, black pepper, paprika, cayenne, garlic, ¼ cup of the parmesan, the lemon juice, vinegar, Worcestershire, Tabasco, mustard, and cream cheese in a food processor and blend until smooth. Transfer to a bowl, add the sour cream, and whisk to combine.

Drain the artichoke hearts and press them lightly to extract any excess moisture. Slice the artichokes crosswise into ¼- to ½-inch slices. Gently fold the artichokes and spinach into the Caesar sauce. Mix well and season to taste with salt. Cover and refrigerate for at least 2 hours, or up to 2 days, before serving.

When you're ready to bake, preheat the oven to 375°F. Scrape the dip into a baking dish and spread it into an even layer. Scatter the remaining ¼ cup parmesan over the top. Bake until bubbling and browned on top, about 15 minutes.

Brush the baguette slices with olive oil and arrange them in a single layer on a baking sheet. Toast in the oven, flipping once, for 4 to 6 minutes total. Serve the dip with the warm toasts.

WHOLE ROASTED CAULIFLOWER

cauliflower, mustard, citrus

Cauliflower and citrus are a really great pairing. Our thought was to take just about every ingredient with citrusy aromas and put them together—the hops in IPA, coriander, honey, lime, and cilantro.

SERVES 4 to 6

COMPOUND
indole

AROMAS
burnt, medicine, mothball

1 head cauliflower

2 tablespoons extra-virgin olive oil FAT

1 teaspoon salt, plus more as needed SALT

½ teaspoon ground coriander

¾ cup India pale ale BITTER, SOUR

1 tablespoon Dijon mustard SPICY

2 teaspoons honey SWEET

1 teaspoon fresh lime juice SOUR

1 tablespoon chopped fresh cilantro

Preheat the oven to 375°F.

Keeping the head of cauliflower intact, trim the stem from the bottom so that the head will sit flat in a baking dish. Coat the outside of the cauliflower with the oil.

This is best done by getting your hands dirty. Drizzle the oil all over the cauliflower, then use your hands to rub it into all of the nooks and crannies.

In a small bowl, mix together the salt and coriander. Sprinkle evenly over the cauliflower. Place the cauliflower in an 8 x 8- or 9 x 9-inch baking dish and pour the beer around the sides to cover the base of the pan.

Tightly cover the pan with aluminum foil and bake for 30 minutes. After 30 minutes, remove the foil and bake for about 20 minutes more.

While the cauliflower is cooking, combine the mustard, honey, lime juice, and a pinch of salt in a small bowl. Mix until smooth.

After the cauliflower has cooked for 20 minutes uncovered, remove it from the oven and brush the surface with the honey-mustard mixture (you may not use it all). Return to the oven and bake for 15 minutes more.

After 15 minutes, check the cauliflower for doneness: The tip of a knife should easily pierce through the center of the cauliflower. If it does not, keep checking at 5-minute intervals until the knife easily passes through.

When the cauliflower is done, brush another layer of the mustard mixture over the cauliflower and transfer it to a plate to rest for 5 minutes.

Scatter the cilantro over the cauliflower and serve.

BROCCOLI WITH PISTACHIO PESTO

broccoli, pistachios, basil

File this under our monochromatic phase—broccoli, basil, pistachios, olive oil, arugula—green on green on green . . . on green. Alpha-pinene is the compound that gives pistachios their unique flavor. It is also prevalent in dark green vegetables such as broccoli and arugula. The pine nuts in traditional pesto are also high in alpha-pinene, so you can try a simpler combination of roasted broccoli and store-bought pesto garnished with chopped pistachios.

SERVES 4

COMPOUND
alpha-pinene

AROMAS
cedar, pine, resin, sharp, turpentine

PESTO

1 cup shelled unsalted pistachios FAT

1 clove garlic, peeled UMAMI

2 tablespoons grated parmesan cheese FAT, SALT, UMAMI

2 cups fresh basil leaves

¾ cup good-quality extra-virgin olive oil, plus more as needed FAT

BROCCOLI

2 heads broccoli (about 1 pound each) BITTER

2 tablespoons vegetable oil, plus more as needed FAT

1 teaspoon kosher salt SALT

½ teaspoon granulated garlic

1 cup arugula leaves, for garnish BITTER, SPICY

Shaved parmesan cheese, for garnish FAT, SALT, UMAMI

½ lemon SOUR

Make the pesto: Combine the pistachios, garlic, and parmesan cheese in a food processor. Blend on high until a smooth paste forms. Add the basil and process in short bursts until the basil is finely chopped. Transfer to a bowl and stir in the olive oil, adding more if needed to form a smooth sauce. Store in the refrigerator in an airtight container for up to 1 week.

Make the broccoli: Preheat the oven to 425°F.

Peel the broccoli stems and slice off ½ to 1 inch from the bottoms of the stalk to remove any tough, fibrous portion. Cut each head of broccoli in half lengthwise, through the stem. Brush the cut side of the broccoli with vegetable oil and season with the salt and garlic powder. Arrange the pieces on a baking sheet cut side down and brush the stem and florets with the remaining oil. Roast until the edges are crisped and brown and the stems are tender, about 18 minutes. Cool briefly on the pan.

To serve, place two large spoonfuls of pesto in the center of each plate and spread it around with the back of a spoon. Place half a broccoli head in the center of each plate. Scatter a few leaves of arugula and shavings of parmesan over each plate. Squeeze a few drops of lemon juice over each plate and serve immediately.

Adding lemon at the last moment will balance the rich pesto and preserve the brilliant green color in the dish.

EGGPLANT DIP

yogurt, dill, sesame, pomegranate, eggplant

Both pomegranate and eggplant have a pleasant bitterness and take well to sour and dairy flavors. Yogurt is an excellent bridge between the two ingredients; here it helps to make things creamy and gives just the right amount of tart. Enjoy this as a dip with vegetables or pita chips or as a spread on pita sandwiches, or serve it with roasted fish or meats.

SERVES 6

COMPOUND
beta-bergamotene

AROMA
tea

2 large eggplant BITTER

1 head roasted garlic (see note) SWEET, UMAMI

1½ teaspoons smoked paprika

2 teaspoons kosher salt SALT

¼ cup extra-virgin olive oil, plus more as needed FAT

¼ cup Greek yogurt FAT, SOUR

2 tablespoons chopped fresh dill, plus more as needed

2 teaspoons toasted sesame seeds

2 tablespoons pomegranate seeds BITTER, SWEET

Preheat the broiler. Adjust the oven rack to the center position.

Place the eggplants on a baking sheet and broil until all sides are well charred, turning them as the skin blackens, 4 to 6 minutes per side. Remove from the oven and let cool.

When the eggplants are cool enough to handle, pull off the charred stem and split each one open. Scoop the flesh away from the skin with a spoon. Place the eggplant flesh in a colander and press lightly to extract any excess liquid. Discard the skins.

Transfer the eggplant flesh to a food processor. Squeeze the roasted garlic cloves out of their skins into the food processor, then add the smoked paprika, salt, and olive oil. Purée until smooth. Transfer the purée to a bowl and press plastic wrap onto the surface. Refrigerate until cooled, at least 2 hours or for up to 2 days.

Add the yogurt and dill and whisk until smooth. To serve, drizzle the top with olive oil and sprinkle with sesame seeds, pomegranate seeds, and more dill.

You can also do this on a hot grill. The goal is to completely blacken the skin, which will give the flesh a nice smoky flavor.

———

To roast garlic: Cut the top (about ⅛ inch) off a whole head of garlic, so the cloves are just exposed. Drizzle the exposed cloves with olive oil and season with salt and pepper. Wrap the garlic in aluminum foil—making it look like a large, fat Hershey's Kiss—and bake in the oven at 350°F until very aromatic and golden brown inside, about 40 minutes. When cool enough to handle, squeeze the head of garlic from the root end to pop the roasted cloves out of the top.

SQUASH SKEWERS

squash, bacon, carrot, vinegar

Even though the cooked carrots and squash in these skewers look similar, each retains its own unique character—the carrot firm and slightly sweet, the squash tender and lightly bitter—and they accentuate the supporting ingredients in different ways. Plus, bacon = yum.

SERVES 4 to 6

COMPOUND
4-vinylguaiacol

AROMAS
clove, curry,
smoke, spice

2 teaspoons olive oil FAT

3 medium carrots, peeled and cut into 1¹/₂-inch pieces (2 cups) SWEET

¹/₄ pound thick-cut bacon, cut into 2-inch pieces FAT, SALT, UMAMI

1 teaspoon ground ginger SPICY

1 teaspoon kosher salt, plus more as needed SALT

Pinch of red pepper flakes SPICY

2 cups peeled, seeded, and chopped butternut squash, 1¹/₂-inch cubes (about ¹/₂ medium squash) SWEET

¹/₂ teaspoon smoked paprika

1 tablespoon red wine vinegar SOUR

1 tablespoon chopped fresh basil leaves

¹/₄ cup crumbled feta cheese FAT, SALT, SOUR, UMAMI

Preheat the oven to 425°F. Line a baking sheet with aluminum foil.

Place the oil, carrots, bacon, ginger, salt, and pepper flakes in a bowl and toss well to coat. Transfer to the baking sheet and spread in a single even layer.

Roast for 6 minutes. Remove the baking sheet from the oven, add the squash, and mix well with a spatula to coat it. Return to the oven and roast for another 6 minutes, until the squash is just tender. It should have only a slight resistance when pierced with a knife. Remove from the oven and set aside to cool slightly.

When the vegetables are cool enough to handle, arrange the vegetables and bacon on skewers in alternating patterns. Make sure not to place them too close together. If they touch one another, they may not cook completely through. You can assemble the skewers up to 24 hours in advance and store them, covered, in the refrigerator.

Preheat the broiler or heat a grill to hot and oil the grates.

Season the skewers with the salt and smoked paprika. Broil or grill 3 to 4 minutes per side, flipping them once, until hot through and browned at the edges. Arrange the skewers on a platter or individual plates and sprinkle with the vinegar, basil, and feta.

Add a bit more oil along with the squash if needed to coat evenly.

If using wooden skewers, soak the skewers in room temperature water for 30 minutes or up to overnight to prevent them from burning when on the grill.

PUMPKIN PILAF

jalapeño, cinnamon, fennel seeds, pumpkin

Jalapeño and pumpkin are flat-out delicious together. It also just so happens that they both pair really well with warm spices like cinnamon and fennel. Pilaf is a style of cooking of grains commonly used for rice, but here we swap out the rice for something heartier. Fregola is a small pasta from Sardinia, little balls of semolina dough that are roasted as part of the drying process, giving them a delicious flavor and distinctive chew. If you can't find fregola, Israeli couscous is a fine substitute.

SERVES 4 to 6

COMPOUND
phenethyl alcohol

AROMAS
fruit, honey, lilac, rose, wine

2 tablespoons unsalted butter FAT

2 cloves garlic, peeled and smashed UMAMI

2 cups diced peeled, seeded pumpkin, acorn squash, or butternut squash SWEET

½ jalapeño chile, seeded and minced SPICY

½ teaspoon fresh thyme leaves or ¼ teaspoon dried thyme

1 teaspoon kosher salt, plus more as needed SALT

1 cinnamon stick

½ teaspoon fennel seeds

2 cups fregola or Israeli couscous

4 cups chicken or vegetable stock UMAMI **or water**

¼ cup grated pecorino or parmesan cheese FAT, SALT, UMAMI

Toasted pumpkin seeds, for garnish (optional)

Melt the butter in a medium saucepot over medium-high heat. As the butter melts, add the garlic and cook until it begins to sizzle and brown lightly around the edges. Stir in the pumpkin, jalapeño, and thyme. Season with the salt and sauté for 2 to 3 minutes, until the pumpkin begins to soften.

Add the cinnamon, fennel seeds, and fregola, stir well, and cook, stirring constantly, for 1 minute. When the spices become aromatic, pour in the stock and bring to a boil. Taste the liquid for salt.

Place a lid on the pot or cover with aluminum foil and reduce the heat to low. Simmer gently until all of the liquid is absorbed, about 15 minutes. Do not stir the pot at any point during the simmering time.

Remove the pot from the heat. Gently stir the pilaf from the bottom up in a folding motion to bring the pasta from the bottom to the top of the pot. Replace the lid and let stand for 5 minutes before serving.

Serve topped with the pecorino and the pumpkin seeds (if using).

It should taste like a fully seasoned soup at this point—as the couscous cooks, it will absorb the majority of the salt from cooking liquid. If the liquid is not seasoned enough the cooked pasta will remain bland, no matter how much salt you add after cooking.

Stirring will release starches from the pasta and make your finished dish more like risotto than a fluffy pilaf.

SCALLOPED PARSNIPS

parsnip, lemon, cream

The old standby of potatoes, cream, and cheese is always going to be good. But we wanted to transform that classic into something more suited for the grown-ups' table. Parsnip is an underappreciated root vegetable with a sweet, earthy flavor. Lemon is a great match for parsnips and dairy, but the acid in lemon juice would cause the creamy sauce to curdle, so we brighten things up with just the zest.

SERVES 6

COMPOUND
terpinolene

AROMAS
pine, sweet, plastic

2 pounds parsnips SWEET, UMAMI

1 pound Yukon gold potatoes UMAMI

2 cups chicken or vegetable stock UMAMI

2 cups half-and-half FAT

2 teaspoons kosher salt SALT

1 clove garlic, peeled and smashed UMAMI

1 bay leaf

Grated zest of 1 lemon

Pinch of freshly grated nutmeg

¼ cup grated parmesan cheese FAT, SALT, UMAMI

½ cup grated sharp cheddar cheese FAT, SALT, UMAMI

Peel the parsnips and cut them into ⅛- to ¼-inch-thick slices using a mandoline or sharp knife. Peel the potatoes and cut them to the same thickness; set them aside separately.

Combine the parsnips, stock, half-and-half, salt, garlic, and bay leaf in a large pot and bring to a boil. When the parsnips reach a boil, stir in the potatoes and return to a boil. As soon as the pot boils, remove it from the heat and add the lemon zest and nutmeg. Cover the pot and let stand for 5 minutes, then remove the bay leaf and transfer the mixture to a 9 x 9-inch baking dish. Spread the vegetables into even layers and scatter the parmesan and cheddar over the top. Cover the baking dish with aluminum foil and bake for 20 minutes.

Remove the foil and bake for 20 to 25 minutes longer, until the sauce is bubbling and the cheese browned. Let cool for 10 minutes before serving.

Nutmeg is always best when grated from a whole seed. Two or three scrapes down the length of a Microplane will add the perfect amount. Whole nutmeg will last much longer in your spice cabinet. Preground nutmeg can lose its potent aroma very quickly, so it is extremely important to give nutmeg the "sniff test" before using.

SUMMER SQUASH GRATIN

squash, tomato, mint, ricotta

We call this a gratin, but it's more like a light, fresh summer vegetable lasagna. Lightly roasting the squash and tomatoes before assembling the dish helps to eliminate excess moisture and gives the vegetables a meatier texture, so they stand up to the second baking. We love the pairing of zucchini and mint, but basil is equally delicious here. This recipe is a great base for all seasons—we've been to know to make it with asparagus in spring or roasted squash and caramelized onions in fall.

SERVES 6

COMPOUND
toluene

AROMAS
glue, paint, solvent

3 Roma tomatoes, sliced
¾ inch thick UMAMI

2 yellow summer squash, sliced
¾ inch thick

2 green zucchini, sliced
¾ inch thick

1 tablespoon minced garlic
UMAMI

2 teaspoons kosher salt SALT

½ teaspoon freshly ground
black pepper SPICY

1 cup ricotta cheese FAT

1 large egg UMAMI

¼ cup milk FAT

1 tablespoon chopped
fresh mint

¼ cup grated parmesan
cheese FAT, SALT, UMAMI

Preheat the oven to 425°F.

Combine the tomatoes, yellow squash, and zucchini in a large bowl with the garlic, salt, and pepper and toss to coat evenly.

Spread the vegetables on two rimmed baking sheets, making sure that they are in a single layer and not crowded on the pans. Roast for 6 minutes, until the zucchini and squash are softened and just tender, then set aside to cool. Leave the oven on.

While the vegetables roast, combine the ricotta, egg, and milk in a bowl and whisk until smooth.

When the vegetables are cool enough to handle, arrange half of the yellow squash, zucchini, and tomatoes in a 9 x 9-inch or similar-size baking dish in overlapping rows. Scatter the mint over the vegetables, then spread two-thirds of the ricotta mixture over the vegetables. Tile the remaining vegetables on top of the ricotta, then spread the remaining ricotta over them and scatter the parmesan over the top.

Bake again until bubbling on the edges, about 12 minutes. Cool slightly before serving.

The point of roasting the vegetables is to eliminate excess moisture. If they are too close to one another, they will steam and become soggy.

Grains and Pasta

All grains are made up of three basic parts: hull/bran, endosperm, and germ. The hull and bran are the edible outer seed covering. Bran adds a significant amount of nutrition to grains in the form of fiber. The endosperm makes up the bulk of a grain and contains mostly stored starches and small amounts of protein. The small kernel known as the germ is the nutritional powerhouse of grain. Like the yolk of an egg, it contains nutrients, protein, and trace amounts of unsaturated fat.

For better nutrition, shop for whole grains, since refined grains such as white rice and products made with white flour (white bread, pasta, crackers, etc.) are made by removing the bran and germ from the grain, thus stripping it of all nutritional value.

GRAIN STRUCTURE

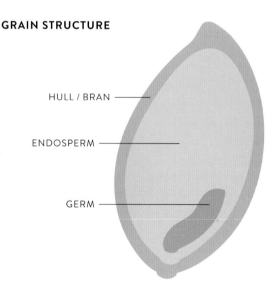

HULL / BRAN

ENDOSPERM

GERM

Cooking Grains

The simplest way to cook grains is to boil them in a lot of water, as you would cook pasta. Bring a large pot of lightly salted water to a boil and stir in the grain. If cooking quinoa, be sure to rinse it thoroughly before cooking. Reduce the heat to a simmer and cook until the grain is tender; see the chart below for cooking times for some of our favorites. Drain the cooked grain in a fine-mesh strainer and serve as desired. Dry grains or pasta can also be added to a soup or stew as it simmers, or cooked risotto-style by gradually adding liquid and frequently stirring as they simmer. Cooking risotto style is a particularly underrated technique for pasta, as this method captures all starches released during the cooking process and holds them in the sauce. We employ this technique in our Sweet Pea and Mushroom Rigatoni Carbonara on page 68.

However you choose to cook your grains or pasta, the one thing that does not change is the need for salt. Grains must begin cooking in a salted liquid. Throughout the cooking the process, the dried starches found inside of grains or pasta begin to soften by bonding with water molecules. This process is your one opportunity to get salt to the *interior* of the grain, which creates a properly seasoned bite. If salt is not introduced in the beginning, then you can only season the exterior of the grain, meaning each bite will always taste underseasoned.

GENERAL COOKING TIMES FOR GRAINS

Fresh pasta	3 to 4 minutes
Dried pasta	8 to 10 minutes
Quinoa	12 to 15 minutes
Teff	12 to 15 minutes
Freekeh (cracked)	20 minutes
Freekeh (whole)	40 minutes
Brown Rice	40 minutes
Farro	45 minutes
Spelt	45 minutes

SPRING VEGETABLE, BROWN BUTTER, AND LEMON PASTA

brown butter, peas, lemon

Many of the recipes in this section explore the extremely strong affinity between green vegetal aromas and deep roasted aromas. This can be a bit of a challenging pairing because green aromas are typically lost in the roasting process, meaning you often get one or the other. But this flavorful pasta highlights both. The best part is that once everything is prepped, the sauce can be made in the same time that it takes the pasta to cook.

SERVES 4

COMPOUND
acetaldehyde

AROMAS
ether, floral, green apple, pungent

1 medium zucchini

1 pound long pasta (such as bucatini, perciatelli, or thick spaghetti)

8 tablespoons (1 stick) unsalted butter FAT

¼ pound pancetta, diced SALT, UMAMI

1 bunch scallions, thinly sliced (green and white parts, about 1 cup)

2 cups fresh green peas (about 2 pounds in the pods) SWEET

Kosher salt, to taste SALT

Freshly ground black pepper, to taste SPICY

Grated zest and juice of 1 lemon SOUR

½ cup grated pecorino or parmesan cheese, plus more for garnish FAT, SALT, UMAMI

Cut the zucchini into thin matchsticks (julienne) using a mandoline, julienne peeler, or spiralizer. Alternatively, grate it on a box grater. You should get about 1½ cups squash. Lightly salt the zucchini and set it aside in a colander in the sink to drain.

Bring a large pot of salted water to a rapid boil. Add the pasta and stir immediately to avoid sticking or clumping. Stir occasionally as the pasta cooks, about 8 minutes total.

Meanwhile, melt the butter in a large sauté pan over high heat. When the butter is fully melted, reduce the heat to medium. Watch the pan carefully as the milk solids begin to toast and the butter takes on an amber color, after about 6 minutes. Immediately add the pancetta and stir well. Continue cooking over medium heat until the pancetta is crisp and browned, 4 to 6 minutes more.

Whichever method of cutting you choose, make sure you cut or grate only the outer colored and fleshy portions of the squash; stop cutting once you reach the seeds in the center. This inner core has a looser texture that becomes mushy and wet when cooked. The outer portion of zucchini and other summer squash are firmer and better suited for cooking.

continued

You could make this meat-less by using diced portabella mushrooms instead of pancetta. Follow the same preparation we use in Rigatoni alla Gricia (page 59)

Add the scallions and sauté for about 30 seconds, until aromatic and tender. Stir in the zucchini and peas and sauté for about 1 minute more. Season to taste with salt and pepper. Stir in 1 cup water from the pasta pot and bring to a boil.

At this point, the pasta should be ready. Transfer the pasta to the sauté pan and simmer for 1 minute more. Remove the pan from the heat and stir in the lemon zest and juice and the pecorino. Stir well for 30 seconds to emulsify the sauce. Serve immediately, garnished with additional cheese.

It is essential to have all of your ingredients fully prepared so that you can add the next as soon as the previous item is cooked. The goal is to get each of the vegetables quickly cooked and tender, but not browned. If you see signs of browning on the vegetables, quickly add the next ingredient to help cool the pan and stop the browning.

CREAMED KALE AND CARAMELIZED ONION MAC AND CHEESE

pasta, kale, caramelized onion

This is a rich and satisfying dish to make for a crowd, full of deep roasted and green aromas. We love it just the way it is, but you can also experiment with seasonal variations—add cut cherry tomatoes or artichokes in summer or diced squash in fall and winter.

SERVES 6

COMPOUND
dimethyl trisulfide

AROMAS
cabbage, fish, onion, sulfur, sweat

4 tablespoons vegetable oil FAT

2 yellow onions, thinly sliced (about 4 cups)

¼ cup all-purpose flour, or a gluten-free alternative

1 tablespoon granulated garlic

4 cups milk FAT

1 pound short tube pasta (such as rigatoni or penne)

1 large bunch kale, stems removed, leaves chopped
BITTER

1 teaspoon vinegar-based hot sauce (such as Tabasco or Crystal) SPICY

2 cups grated cheddar or Gruyère cheese UMAMI

1½ cups grated parmesan cheese FAT, SALT, UMAMI

Heat 2 tablespoons of the oil in a Dutch oven over high heat until it begins to lightly smoke around the edges. Add all of the onions at once and stir well. Cook for 30 seconds, then reduce the heat to medium-low and continue cooking, stirring occasionally, until the onions are tender and brown, 30 to 40 minutes. If the onions are still light in the center but dark at the edges, reduce the heat further and continue to cook. The goal is to cook them slow and low so that they brown evenly, becoming tender and sweet.

Add the remaining 2 tablespoons oil to the pot and stir in the flour and garlic. Cook for 1 minute, scraping the bottom of the pan and breaking up any lumps. Turn the heat to high and add the milk 1 cup at a time, stirring constantly and taking care to scrape the bottom and the corners of the pot to prevent scorching. Allow each addition to come to a boil before adding the next. When all the milk has been added, reduce the heat to medium and simmer for about 5 minutes, until the sauce is thick and smooth.

Meanwhile, bring a large pot of salted water to a boil and cook the pasta al dente according to the package instructions. Drain it well.

Properly caramelizing onions takes time. Be patient and do not try to rush it. If the onions are cooked too quickly they will burn on the outside and remain pungent in the center. When done right, caramelized onions should be creamy and sweet throughout.

—

Adding the milk gradually ensures you will not get lumps in your sauce.

continued

Stir the kale and hot sauce into the onion sauce and simmer for about 5 minutes more. Remove the pot from the heat and stir in the cheddar and 1 cup of the parmesan.

Add the drained pasta and stir well to coat. Transfer the mixture to a 13 x 9-inch baking dish. At this point you can let the pasta cool, then refrigerate it for up to 2 days, tightly covered.

Preheat the oven to 425°F.

Just before baking, top with the remaining ½ cup parmesan. Bake until golden brown on top and bubbling, about 15 minutes. If baking directly from the refrigerator, add 10 minutes to cook time. Let cool for about 5 minutes before serving.

RIGATONI ALLA GRICIA WITH MUSHROOM "PANCETTA"

mushrooms, maple syrup, soy sauce, vinegar

Here we have a lineup of perfectly flavor-matched ingredients as well as sweet, sour, salt, and umami working in harmony. The result is shiitake mushrooms that act and taste just like crisp bacon in our vegetarian take on the classic Roman pasta dish.

SERVES 4

COMPOUND
2,3,5-trimethyl-pyrazine

AROMAS
cocoa, earth, must, potato, roast

2 tablespoons soy sauce SALT, UMAMI

2 teaspoons maple syrup SWEET

1 teaspoon red wine vinegar SOUR

1 pound shiitake mushrooms, cleaned, stems removed and discarded, sliced UMAMI

8 ounces rigatoni pasta

2 tablespoons extra-virgin olive oil FAT

¼ cup grated pecorino cheese, plus more for serving FAT, SALT, UMAMI

Combine the soy sauce, maple syrup, and vinegar in a bowl and whisk to combine. Add the mushroom caps and toss well to coat. Leave to marinate at room temperature for 15 minutes, or refrigerate, covered, up to overnight.

Bring a pot of salted water to a boil and cook the rigatoni according to the package instructions. When the pasta is done, reserve 1 cup of the cooking water before draining the pasta.

Drain the mushrooms well, reserving the marinade, and pat them dry. Heat the olive oil in a large sauté pan over high heat. When the oil begins to shimmer, add the mushrooms to the pan. Quickly spread them in an even layer and sear them, without stirring, for 1 to 2 minutes, until they are crisp on one side. Stir well and cook 1 to 2 minutes more, until browned on all sides. Add the reserved marinade and continue cooking until all of the liquid has been completely absorbed, about 1 minute more.

Add the cooked pasta and reserved pasta cooking water to the pan and toss well. Cook for 1 minute, then remove the pan from the heat, add the cheese, and stir well. Divide between bowls and top with more cheese.

The maple syrup and soy sauce will mimic the salt-and-sugar balance of cured pancetta, while the vinegar will soften the mushrooms and keep them from tasting too sweet. These ingredients will also help the mushrooms develop a brown and crispy exterior like pancetta when cooked.

QUINOA SALAD

hazelnuts, vinegar, sweet potato, honey

Honey has a particular affinity for grains, while the vinegar in this recipe balances the sweetness. We strongly recommend making this vinaigrette in big batches and keeping a jar of it in the fridge. It is great for a simple green salad, and can really take a fresh fruit salad to the next level—it's excellent with watermelon, grapes, cantaloupe, and apples.

SERVES 4 as main, 8 as a side

COMPOUND acetyl propionyl

AROMAS butter, caramel, cream, fruit, sweet

HONEY VINAIGRETTE

¼ cup apple cider vinegar SOUR

1 tablespoon honey SWEET

1 tablespoon minced shallot

1 teaspoon Dijon mustard SPICY

½ teaspoon fresh thyme leaves

¼ cup extra-virgin olive oil FAT

QUINOA

2 cups quinoa

2 medium sweet potatoes, sliced into rounds SWEET

Kosher salt SALT

Freshly ground black pepper SPICY

2 tablespoons extra-virgin olive oil FAT

2 cloves garlic, halved UMAMI

½ cup chopped hazelnuts FAT

Small greens like arugula, watercress, or baby kale, for garnish (optional) BITTER

Shaved parmesan or pecorino cheese or crumbled feta or goat cheese, for garnish (optional) FAT, SALT, UMAMI

Make the honey vinaigrette: Combine the vinegar, honey, shallot, mustard, thyme, and oil in a small bowl and stir well to combine. Set aside until needed. You can triple or quadruple the recipe and store it in the refrigerator in a covered container for up to 2 weeks. Whisk or stir it to recombine before using.

Make the quinoa: Bring a pot of salted water to a boil. While the water heats, rinse the quinoa thoroughly in a fine-mesh strainer under running water. Add the quinoa to the boiling water and stir well. Reduce the heat a strong simmer and cook for 10 to 14 minutes, until the quinoa is just tender and no white dots are visible in the center of the grain.

When the quinoa is cooked, drain it in a fine-mesh strainer and spread it out on a baking sheet to steam-dry.

Preheat the oven to 425°F or heat a grill to medium-high and oil the grates.

Brush the slices of sweet potato on both sides with the honey vinaigrette. Then season lightly with salt and pepper.

To cook the sweet potatoes in the oven, arrange them on a baking sheet in a single layer without touching. Divide between two baking sheets if necessary; overcrowding will prevent the sweet potatoes from browning. Roast until tender, 12 to 16 minutes.

continued

A thorough rinsing before cooking will prevent the cooked quinoa from tasting too bitter.

Season the potatoes immediately before placing them in the oven or on the grill. If the salt sits on the sweet potatoes too long, it will draw water to the surface and they'll end up steaming, not browning.

To cook the sweet potatoes on the grill, arrange them flat on the grill and cook for about 2 minutes, then rotate them 90 degrees and cook for 2 minutes more. Flip and repeat on the second side. If the sweet potatoes are not tender through, continue cooking, flipping the pieces every minute until they are done.

Set the cooked sweet potatoes aside to cool slightly before serving. The sweet potatoes may be prepared in advance, up to 24 hours, and either reheated or served at room temperature.

Assemble the salad: Combine the oil, garlic, and hazelnuts in a large nonstick sauté pan over medium heat. Cook until the garlic begins to sizzle and brown around the edges. Immediately add the quinoa and stir once to coat. Turn the heat to high and cook undisturbed until the quinoa starts to "pop." Remove the pan from the heat. Serve the quinoa with the roasted sweet potatoes, drizzled with some of the vinaigrette, and garnished with greens and cheese (if desired).

FARRO AND CRISPY KALE SALAD

wheat, bell pepper, tomato, feta

Lactones are a group of aromatics that have floral and tropical fruit aromas. You might not be surprised to find them in tomatoes and pepper, but grains and cheese contain an unexpected amount of lactones as well. In addition, smoky aromas created during the cooking process match with aromas naturally present in cooked grains to create delicious layers of flavors along with the unique textures in this salad.

SERVES 4

COMPOUND
4-hydroxypenta-noic acid lactone

AROMAS
herb, sweet, floral

1 cup farro

1 teaspoon kosher salt, plus more to taste SALT

Grated zest and juice of 1 lemon SOUR

6 tablespoons extra-virgin olive oil FAT

¼ teaspoon smoked paprika

6 cloves garlic, peeled and smashed UMAMI

One 10-ounce bag chopped kale or 1 large bunch, stems removed, chopped BITTER

1 red bell pepper, roasted (see tip), peeled, seeded, and chopped (about 1 cup)

¼ cup coarsely chopped skin-on almonds, lightly toasted (see tip, page 21) FAT, BITTER

½ cup crumbled feta cheese FAT, SALT, SOUR, UMAMI

Freshly ground black pepper SPICY

Combine the farro, 3 cups water, and the salt in a saucepot. Bring to a boil, then reduce the heat to a simmer. Cover the pot and cook for about 25 minutes, until the farro is tender. Drain the farro and transfer it to a large bowl.

Pour the lemon zest and juice, 2 tablespoons of the olive oil, and the paprika over the warm farro and toss to combine. Let cool to room temperature.

In a large sauté pan over high heat, heat 2 tablespoons of the olive oil and half of the garlic. When the garlic begins to brown at the edge, add half of the kale.

Allow the kale to cook undisturbed for 30 seconds, so that the edges begin to get a little crispy. Then gently toss or stir and cook for 30 seconds more. Immediately transfer the kale to the bowl with the farro.

Wipe out the sauté pan with a paper towel and add the remaining 2 tablespoons olive oil and the rest of the garlic. Sauté the second batch of kale and add it to the bowl.

Grains like farro will never get soft; they always a little bite or al dente feel. When cooking farro, you want to ensure that there are no more gritty or chalky raw starches left in the center of the grain.

—

Add the kale carefully: It will sizzle and pop immediately, but that's a good thing as it gives the kale crisp, crunchy edges.

continued

Add the roasted pepper, almonds, and feta. Toss well to combine and adjust the seasoning to taste with salt and pepper.

VARIATION   Try this with buckwheat instead: Thoroughly rinse 1 cup buckwheat kernels in a fine-mesh strainer under running water and drain well. Heat 1 tablespoon oil in a medium saucepot and add the buckwheat. Sauté over high heat for 2 minutes. Add 1½ cups water, cover, and simmer until all the liquid is absorbed, 10 to 12 minutes.

To roast a bell pepper: Place the pepper directly on a gas burner turned to high, or on a hot grill, or on a pan directly below the broiler, and allow the skin to blacken completely before turning with a pair of tongs. Blacken the skin on all sides of the pepper, then transfer it to a bowl and cover with a kitchen towel. Set aside to cool for 10 minutes. Using a slightly damp paper towel, wipe the charred skin from the pepper. Avoid rinsing the pepper under running water; this would literally send all that rich smoky flavor right down the drain. Remove the stem, then cut open the pepper and remove the seeds from the inside.

SUMMER SQUASH VONGOLE

squash, clams, tomato, basil

This a pasta that we make at our restaurant, Angelena's, to celebrate all the glorious summer bounty of the Gulf Coast. It's based on the idea that clams and summer squash are flavor best friends. We also occasionally use this pairing (minus the spaghetti) on pizzas!

SERVES 4

COMPOUND
dimethylamine

AROMA
fish

4 medium yellow summer squash or zucchini

Kosher salt SALT

2 tablespoons olive oil FAT

2 tablespoons unsalted butter FAT

1 tablespoon minced garlic UMAMI

½ cup halved cherry tomatoes UMAMI

50 littleneck clams, well rinsed UMAMI

Juice of ½ lemon SOUR

1 tablespoon chopped fresh basil

Grated pecorino or parmesan cheese, for garnish FAT, SALT, UMAMI

Cut the squash into thin matchsticks (julienne) using a mandoline, julienne peeler, or spiralizer. Alternatively, grate it on a box grater. Lightly salt the squash and set aside in a colander in the sink to drain.

In a large sauté pan, combine 1 tablespoon of the olive oil, 1 tablespoon of the butter and half of the garlic over medium-high heat. When the garlic begins to sizzle, gently squeeze the squash dry with paper towels and add it to the pan. Spread it quickly into an even layer and cook undisturbed for 1 minute. Gently toss and cook for 1 to 2 minutes more, until the squash is tender but still retains a little bite. Transfer the cooked squash to a bowl and return the pan to the heat.

Add the remaining oil, butter, garlic, and the cherry tomatoes to the pan. When the garlic begins to sizzle, add the clams and immediately cover the pan with a tight fitting lid. Simmer for 4 minutes, then check to see that all the clams have opened. If they have not, stir well, replace the lid, and cook for 1 minute before checking again. Continue to cook until all or most of the clams have cooked, up to 7 minutes more. Discard any clams that have not opened.

When all the clams have opened, uncover the pan and simmer for about 1 minute to reduce the clam liquor. Stir in the lemon juice, squash, and basil. Toss well to combine and season to taste with salt.

Divide between bowls, garnish with pecorino, and serve immediately.

Whichever method of cutting you choose, make sure you cut or grate only the outer colored and fleshy portions of the squash. Stop cutting once you reach the seeds in the center. This inner core has a looser texture that becomes mushy and wet when cooked. The outer portion of zucchini and squash are firmer and better suited for cooking.

Cheese will add a little salt and fat that complement the briny clams perfectly. Pecorino, which is made from sheep's milk, is ideal because it adds a little tang, but parmesan is a fine substitute.

SWEET PEA AND MUSHROOM RIGATONI CARBONARA

eggs, sweet peas, mushrooms, wheat

Eggs and peas are a first-ballot Hall of Fame pairing. At Angelena's, we will occasionally toast the flour we are using to make fresh pasta to give it a deeper roasted, nutty flavor. You can achieve this same effect at home by toasting your pasta in a pan before you cook it, as we do in this recipe.

SERVES 6

COMPOUND
cumene

AROMA
solvent

4 large egg yolks FAT, UMAMI

1 cup grated parmesan cheese, plus more for serving FAT, SALT, UMAMI

1 tablespoon unsalted butter FAT

1 tablespoon olive oil FAT

1 pound rigatoni

2 cloves garlic, peeled and smashed UMAMI

8 ounces cremini mushrooms, cleaned and quartered UMAMI

Kosher salt SALT

One 12- to 16-ounce package frozen petit peas or baby sweet peas

Combine the egg yolks and parmesan in a bowl and whisk until smooth; set aside.

Place a large, wide, heavy-bottomed sauté pan over high heat. Add the butter and olive oil. When the butter begins to foam, stir in the dry pasta and reduce the heat to medium-high. Cook the pasta, stirring constantly, until it is toasted and browned in spots, 3 to 4 minutes.

Add the garlic and mushrooms and sauté to soften the mushrooms slightly, another 3 to 4 minutes.

Add 2 cups water and stir well. Adjust the heat so that the liquid is at a strong simmer. Season well with salt.

Continue to cook, stirring occasionally, until nearly all of the water is absorbed. Add more water 1 cup at a time, letting it be absorbed before adding more, until the pasta is tender. This typically takes about 6 cups water total, and about 14 minutes. Make sure to continue tasting and seasoning as the pasta cooks.

Using a combination of butter and olive oil helps achieve the right balance of browning and heat stability.

The best way to clean mushrooms is to quickly dunk them in bowl of room temperature water, swish them around, and immediately transfer to paper towels and pat dry.

Seasoning as you cook is essential. This dish will build a creamy, well-seasoned sauce, but if you do not add salt early on, the pasta will not absorb it and you will be left with a beautiful sauce and bland pasta.

Once the pasta is cooked, and approximately 1 cup of cooking liquid remains in the pot, reduce the heat to low. Stir the peas into the pasta. Simmer until the peas are warmed through, 1 to 2 minutes. Pour in the egg yolk mixture and stir well so that it evenly coats the pasta and begins to thicken slightly. Remove the pan from the heat and continue stirring for 30 seconds to make sure the egg yolks do not curdle.

Serve immediately, topped with more cheese.

You do not want the egg yolks to curdle or become scrambled. Have a small amount of room temperature water on standby. If the eggs yolks get too hot or too thick, stir in a little water to stop them from curdling.

VEGETABLE BOLOGNESE WITH OLIVE GREMOLATA

olives, sage, orange, almonds

This dish is all about subtle surprises. Olives and sage are a classic match for tomato sauce, but almonds and orange are rarely asked to join in. Toasted salted almonds stand in for cheese, providing the same salty and nutty punctuation you would get from parmesan or pecorino, while making this dish vegan. This works because olives and almonds are such a strong pairing, and orange zest matches with the strong fruit aromas in the olives. But of course, it never hurts to finish it all off with a sprinkle of cheese, if you desire.

SERVES 4

COMPOUND
myrcene

AROMAS
balsamic, flower, fruit, herb, must

¼ cup extra-virgin olive oil FAT

1 tablespoon chopped garlic
UMAMI

½ teaspoon red pepper flakes
SPICY

¼ cup diced peeled carrot
SWEET

¼ cup diced celery

½ cup diced onion

Kosher salt SALT

1 tablespoon tomato paste
UMAMI

1 tablespoon soy sauce SALT, UMAMI

1 cup white wine ACID

Heat the olive oil, garlic, and pepper flakes in large saucepot over medium-high heat. Add the carrot, celery, and onions. Season the vegetables with salt and sauté until tender but not browned, about 6 minutes.

While the vegetables cook, combine the tomato paste, soy sauce, and wine and whisk until smooth. Deglaze the pot with the wine mixture and reduce until nearly dry, 1 to 2 minutes.

Add the canned tomatoes and their juices, the sage, basil, and oregano. Bring to a boil and season to taste with salt and black pepper. Reduce the heat to a simmer and cook for about 10 minutes, until the tomatoes begin to break down and the flavors have developed.

Taste the sauce a final time, adjust the seasoning, and add a pinch of sugar if it is too acidic. You can purée the sauce if desired or use it as is. You can store the sauce in a covered container in the refrigerator for up to 2 weeks or freeze it for up to 6 months. If stored, reheat the sauce in a saucepot before proceeding with the recipe.

Mixing the tomato paste with other liquids helps loosen the paste and allows it to more evenly coat the vegetables, providing more depth and flavor.

One 28-ounce can chopped
tomatoes UMAMI

2 branches fresh sage

2 branches fresh basil

2 teaspoons dried oregano

Freshly ground black pepper
SPICY

Sugar (optional) SWEET

1 pound fresh pappardelle, or
a dried pasta shape

¼ teaspoon orange zest
(about 1 full scrape on a
Microplane)

1 tablespoon chopped fresh
flat-leaf parsley

1 tablespoon chopped celery
leaves BITTER

2 tablespoons halved, pitted
niçoise olives SALT, UMAMI

¼ cup chopped toasted
almonds (see tip, page 21) FAT

Bring a large pot of salted water to a rapid boil. Drop the pasta
into the boiling water and stir immediately. Cook, stirring occasionally, until al dente, about 3 minutes for fresh or 8 minutes for
dried, or according to the package directions.

While the pasta cooks, make the gremolata by mixing together
the orange zest, parsley, celery leaves, and olives in a small bowl.

Transfer the cooked pasta to the pot with the sauce and add
½ cup of the pasta cooking water. Bring to a simmer and cook
for about 1 minute, then stir in the almonds. Add more of the
pasta water if the sauce is too thick. Serve the pasta garnished
with the gremolata.

Cheese

Cheese is a near-perfect food on its own—with texture, salt, fat, umami, and complex aromas all in a single bite—yet when combined with other ingredients it only gets better. There are few foods that a little cheese cannot help to improve (on page 236 you will even find cheese incorporated into a sweet dessert). The most amazing thing about this incredibly versatile ingredient, which can be found in thousands of different forms around the world, is that all cheese begins its life as the same thing: milk.

The flavor of a finished cheese is determined by the type of milk used and the steps that milk is taken through during the cheese-making process. We could easily fill volumes on this topic, but we won't. Instead, here's a broad, sweeping look at the basics.

The three most common milks used in cheese making, and their flavors, are:

Cow: mild and milky
Sheep: tangy and salty
Goat: tart

Other factors also affect the ultimate flavor of a finished cheese.

TEMPERATURE

Heat can destroy delicate compounds that give milk flavor. This is why some people ignore sometimes overly cautious food safety rules and prefer unpasteurized cheeses. Even if a cheese is made with unpasteurized milk, the temperature that the milk is heated to during processing will still affect the texture of the curd and the flavor of the cheese. As temperatures increase, or the longer the cheese spends at elevated temperatures, many of compounds responsible for its delicate flavors can be destroyed.

COAGULATING AGENT

Cheese curds are made up of coagulated fat and protein which separates from the liquid part of the milk (the whey). During processing, enzymes and/or acids are added to warm milk to initiate coagulation. These coagulating agents can impart their own flavor to the cheese making process.

INCLUSIONS

Any number of additional ingredients may be incorporated into a cheese during production. These include peppercorns or truffle peelings, or additional bacteria or mold intentionally added for flavor, as in blue cheese.

RINSING

Once the cheese is formed, it may be washed or rinsed to impart unique flavors in the aging process. Beer, wine, and salt brines are the most common rinses.

AGING

The final factor affecting the flavor and texture of the cheese is time. Over months or sometimes years of aging, moisture is lost—making the taste of the cheese more intense—and complex aromas develop, imparting a richer flavor. The loss of moisture in aging also results in drier, more crumbly cheeses.

From a flavor perspective, the dairy aromas found in all cheeses have a particular affinity for floral, tropical fruit, sour, and nutty aromas. The following recipes explore those pairings in a number of different forms.

CHERRY-OLIVE JAM

cherries, olives, wine

Jamie first stumbled upon the combination of cherries and olives as part of a dish he was developing for IBM's Chef Watson project. While his version wound up accompanying duck, Brooke could imagine an even better use: to spread it on crackers to enjoy with mild, creamy cheeses. It is truly the *greatest* condiment for a cheese plate we have ever tasted—beyond the simple appeal of a salty-sweet combo, the way the flavors of these two ingredients come together is indescribable.

MAKES
about 1 cup

COMPOUND
ethanol

AROMAS
alcohol, floral, ripe apple, sweet

½ cup dried sweet cherries
SWEET

1 cup red wine ACID

2 branches fresh sage or ¼ teaspoon dried sage

1 cup pitted niçoise olives, drained, brine saved SALT, UMAMI

Combine the cherries, wine, and sage in a saucepot over medium heat. Bring the mixture to a simmer and cook until about 2 tablespoons liquid remain in the pot, about 8 minutes. Remove from the heat and let rest in the pot for 5 minutes.

Discard the sage (if using fresh). Combine the cherries and olives in a blender and process until smooth, gradually adding small amounts of brine until the mixture is smooth. Store in the refrigerator in an airtight container for up to 2 weeks.

BUFFALO CAULIFLOWER BAKE

cauliflower, blue cheese

Capsicums (peppers and chiles, here in the form of sriracha), alliums, and cheese in general are great matches for cauliflower, but blue cheese in particular is a very strong match. This recipe is kind of like buffalo, ranch, and blue cheese all in one, but with vegetables! It's the ultimate party dish.

SERVES 4 to 6

COMPOUND
methylamine

AROMAS
fish, pungent

1 head cauliflower, cut into florets

2 tablespoons vegetable oil FAT

2 teaspoons Worcestershire sauce UMAMI

1 tablespoon sriracha SPICY

1 teaspoon dried dill

1 teaspoon onion powder

1 teaspoon garlic powder UMAMI

1 teaspoon kosher salt SALT

³⁄₄ cup blue cheese crumbles FAT, SALT, UMAMI

8 ounces cream cheese, softened FAT

¹⁄₂ cup grated parmesan cheese FAT, SALT, UMAMI

¹⁄₂ cup milk FAT

4 scallions (green and white parts), chopped

¹⁄₂ cup diced Roma tomato UMAMI

Crackers or toasted bread, for serving

Celery sticks, for serving

Preheat the oven to 425°F.

In a large bowl, toss together the cauliflower florets, oil, Worcestershire, sriracha, dill, onion powder, garlic powder, and salt. Mix well to coat and transfer to an 8 x 8-inch baking dish.

In the same bowl, combine ¹⁄₂ cup of the blue cheese, the cream cheese, parmesan, and milk. Beat until smooth. Stir in the scallions and tomato, then return the cauliflower to the bowl and mix well.

Transfer the mixture back to the baking dish and spread in an even layer. Scatter the remaining ¹⁄₄ cup blue cheese over the top of the cauliflower and bake for about 30 minutes, until the cauliflower is tender.

Let cool for 5 to 10 minutes before serving with crackers or toasted bread and celery sticks.

You could transfer the cauliflower to another bowl, but this way you'll have fewer dishes to wash.

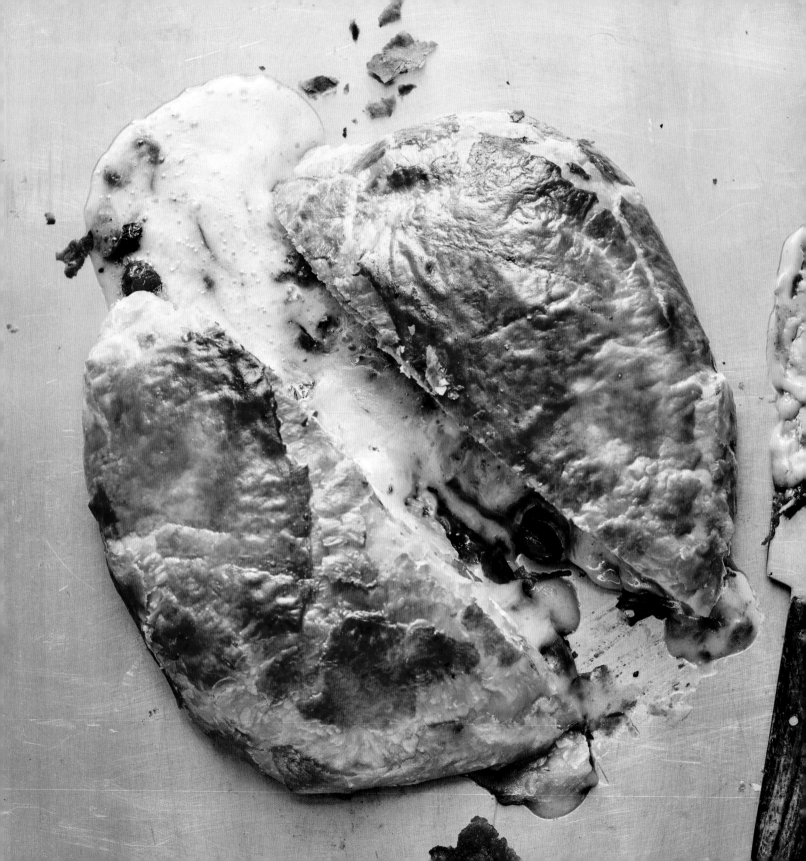

CRANBERRY-STUFFED BAKED BRIE

dairy, cranberries, orange

This is our flavor-forward update to a holiday entertaining classic. It's perfect to prepare in advance and still wow friends and family when it comes hot of the oven. Cranberry, citrus, and Dijon mustard are all great matches for dairy. These ingredients are naturally bitter and acidic, putting them at odds with delicate milk . . . unless it's in the form of cheese. This recipe can be prepared up to the point of just before baking, as much as a day in advance, and refrigerated until you're ready to bake; it can go directly from the refrigerator to the oven. Serve with additional Cranberry Chutney on the side and nuts, dried fruit, and/or crackers.

SERVES 6 to 8

COMPOUND
methyl 2-methyl-butanoate

AROMAS
apple, fruit, green apple, strawberry, sweet

---

1 whole round (about 12 ounces) Brie FAT, UMAMI

½ cup Cranberry Chutney, homemade (recipe follows) or store-bought BITTER, SWEET

1 sheet puff pastry (from a 17.3-ounce package), thawed if frozen

1½ teaspoons Dijon mustard SPICY

All-purpose flour, for dusting

1 large egg, beaten

Line a baking sheet with parchment paper.

Cut the round of Brie in half horizontally, as if splitting a hamburger bun. Lift the top off the Brie and spread the Cranberry Chutney over the bottom half. Replace the top.

Lay the sheet of puff pastry on a lightly floured work surface. Gently roll the pastry with a rolling pin so the dough becomes a square about 12 inches on each side. Spoon the mustard into the center of the pastry. Using a pastry brush, spread into a thin, even layer slightly larger than the Brie. Place the filled Brie in the center of the puff pastry. Cut a piece about 1 inch at its base from each corner of the pastry so that the shape resembles a stop sign.

Fold in the four corners of the puff pastry so they meet in the center of the Brie. Lightly brush the dough where the pieces meet with the egg. Fold the remaining edges into the center so that the Brie is tightly wrapped.

continued

Flip the Brie onto the prepared baking sheet seam side down. Refrigerate for at least 1 hour or up to 1 day; cover loosely with plastic wrap if refrigerating for much longer than 1 hour. Reserve the egg mixture in the refrigerator as well. Use it to brush the entire pastry before placing in the oven.

While the brie is chilling, preheat the oven to 400°F.

Bake until golden brown, about 35 minutes. Let cool on the pan for at least 10 minutes, then use a large spatula to transfer to a serving platter and serve immediately.

CRANBERRY CHUTNEY

One 12-ounce bag fresh or frozen cranberries BITTER, SOUR

1 Granny Smith apple, grated SOUR, SWEET

⅓ cup packed brown sugar SWEET

½ teaspoon ground cinnamon

½ teaspoon ground ginger SPICY

Pinch of ground cloves

Grated zest and juice of 1 orange

Kosher salt SALT

Freshly ground black pepper SPICY

Combine the cranberries, apple, brown sugar, cinnamon, ginger, cloves, orange zest and juice, and ¼ cup water in a saucepot and bring to a boil. Reduce the heat and simmer until thickened, about 20 minutes. Season to taste with salt and pepper. Serve warm or chilled. Store in an airtight container in the refrigerator for up to 2 weeks.

MAKES
about 1 cup

ULTIMATE GRILLED CHEESE SANDWICHES

cheese, bread

The humble grilled cheese is a beautiful sandwich that is all too often relegated to the kids' table. This ain't kid stuff. Here we're going to give you three incredible, grown-up variations.

It all starts with the base cheese mixture. It's leagues above your garden-variety American singles—trust us, you're going to want to make a bunch of it. When you have a container of this sitting in your fridge, you're just a few minutes away from crusty, melty, perfectly balanced grilled cheese sandwiches any time.

MAKES about 4 cups of base, enough for 16 sandwiches

COMPOUND 4-methylpentanoic acid

AROMA floral

ULTIMATE GRILLED CHEESE SANDWICH BASE

2 tablespoons mayonnaise FAT

4 tablespoons cream cheese, softened FAT

1 teaspoon garlic powder UMAMI

1/2 teaspoon paprika (smoked, if you prefer)

2 cup grated cheddar cheese FAT, SALT, UMAMI

1 cup grated provolone cheese FAT, SALT, UMAMI

1/2 cup grated parmesan cheese FAT, SALT, UMAMI

SANDWICHES

2 slices bread per sandwich

Softened unsalted butter or mayonnaise, for cooking FAT

Make the cheese base: Blend together the mayonnaise, cream cheese, garlic powder, and paprika in a medium bowl. Fold in the cheddar, provolone, and parmesan until well mixed. If not using immediately, store in an airtight container in the refrigerator for up to 10 days.

To make a plain grilled cheese sandwich: Spread about 4 tablespoons of the cheese mixture on one slice of bread and top with the other slice. Spread butter or mayonnaise on the outside of the bread. Heat a cast-iron skillet or nonstick sauté pan over medium heat. Add the sandwich to the pan, press it lightly with a spatula, and leave it to cook until golden brown on the bottom, about 3 minutes. Flip the sandwich and brown on the second side, another 2 to 3 minutes. Let the sandwich cool slightly before cutting.

Cooking a perfect grilled cheese requires the perfect heat. Too high heat will mean extra crispy (read: burnt) bread before the cheese inside reaches full, melty goodness. Too low means bread that's dry and pale rather than buttery, crisp, and golden brown. Preheating a cast-iron pan is essential. Allow the pan to heat on medium-low for at least 3 minutes before adding the sandwich, to ensure even heat distribution.

SPICY KIWI AND BACON GRILLED CHEESE SANDWICHES

kiwi, jalapeño, bacon

This sandwich is all about the balance of sweet, spicy, and salty, so proportions matter. Make sure the cheese is spread in an even layer, and arrange the kiwi slices so that they are not overlapping at all. They will not cover all of the cheese, but they don't need to.

MAKES
4 sandwiches

COMPOUND
3-carene

AROMAS
bell pepper, lemon, resin, rubber

8 slices bread

1 cup Ultimate Grilled Cheese Sandwich Base (page 79) FAT, SALT, UMAMI

2 ripe kiwi, peeled and thinly sliced SWEET

½ jalapeño chile, sliced into rings SPICY

8 slices bacon, cooked until crisp (save the rendered fat, if you like) FAT, SALT, UMAMI

Softened butter, mayonnaise, or reserved bacon fat, for cooking FAT

Place 4 slices bread on a cutting board. Spread about 2 tablespoons of the cheese mixture on each slice of bread. Arrange 3 or 4 slices of kiwi on top of the cheese. Scatter a few jalapeño slices over the kiwi, then top with 2 slices bacon on each sandwich. Break the bacon into pieces if it overhangs the sandwich edges too much.

Spread 2 tablespoons of the cheese mixture on each of the remaining 4 slices bread and close the sandwiches, pressing the cheese onto the bacon.

Preheat a cast-iron skillet or nonstick sauté pan over medium heat for 3 to 4 minutes. Spread both sides of each sandwich with butter or mayonnaise and (Alternatively, leave the sandwich uncoated and heat 1 tablespoon bacon fat in the pan.) Add the sandwich to the pan, press it lightly with a spatula, and leave it to cook until golden brown on the bottom, about 3 minutes. Flip the sandwich and brown on the second side, another 2 to 3 minutes. Let the sandwich cool slightly before cutting. Repeat with the other sandwiches.

BROCCOLI AND KIMCHI GRILLED CHEESE SANDWICHES

kimchi, broccoli, cheddar

Sulphur compounds are known for creating deep, rich, and somewhat funky aromas in foods, boiled eggs being one most the pure examples. But don't let that scare you off—the sulphur compounds shared between broccoli and kimchi are delicious in the best possible way. In fact, if you want to take this sandwich to the next level, we strongly encourage you top it off with a fried egg.

MAKES
4 sandwiches

COMPOUND
dimethyl trisulfide

AROMAS
cabbage, fish, onion, sulphur

¼ cup kimchi, drained UMAMI, SPICY

2 cups chopped raw broccoli (about 1 small head, including the stem) BITTER

8 slices bread

1 cup Ultimate Grilled Cheese Sandwich Base (page 79) FAT, SALT, UMAMI

Softened butter or mayonnaise, for cooking FAT

Combine the kimchi and broccoli in a food processor. Pulse in 3-second bursts to chop and mix well. Transfer to a strainer and set aside to drain for 5 minutes

Place 4 slices bread on a cutting board. Spread about 2 tablespoons of the cheese mixture on each slice of bread. Divide the broccoli mixture evenly between the sandwiches.

Spread about 2 tablespoons of the cheese mixture on each of the remaining 4 slices bread, then close the sandwiches, pressing the cheese onto the broccoli mixture on the bottom halves.

Preheat a cast-iron skillet or nonstick pan over medium heat for 3 to 4 minutes. Spread both sides of each sandwich with butter or mayonnaise. Add the sandwich to the pan, press it lightly with a spatula, and leave it to cook until golden brown on the bottom, about 3 minutes. Flip the sandwich and brown on the second side, another 2 to 3 minutes. Let cool slightly before cutting. Repeat with the remaining sandwiches.

HAM AND APPLE GRILLED CHEESE SANDWICHES

olives, apple, pork

MAKES
4 sandwiches

COMPOUND
1-heptanol

AROMAS
chemical, green, wood

Pork and apple are an all-time classic pairing. That's due in part to the compound 1-heptanol, which has chemical, green aromas and just happens to be prominent in olives and mustard as well, adding a little spice and saltiness to an already great combo.

8 slices olive sourdough bread UMAMI

2 tablespoons Dijon mustard SPICY

8 slices smoked ham (about 2 ounces) UMAMI

½ apple, thinly sliced SWEET

1 cup Ultimate Grilled Cheese Sandwich Base (page 79) FAT, SALT, UMAMI

Extra-virgin olive oil, for cooking FAT

Place 4 slices bread on a cutting board. Spread ½ tablespoon mustard on each slice. Fold the ham slices so that two slices overlap slightly and are the same size as the bread. Place on top of the mustard and top the ham with apple slices.

Divide the cheese mixture between the remaining 4 slices bread and spread into an even layer. Close the sandwiches, pressing the cheese into the apples.

Preheat a cast-iron skillet or nonstick pan over medium heat for 3 to 4 minutes. Add just enough olive oil to coat the bottom of the pan. Carefully place a sandwich in the pan, press it lightly with a spatula, and leave it to cook until golden brown on the bottom, about 3 minutes. Flip the sandwich and brown on the second side, another 2 to 3 minutes. Let cool slightly before cutting. Repeat with the remaining sandwiches, adding fresh olive oil with each sandwich.

ULTIMATE BLT WITH "TO-MAYO"

bacon, tomato

We're aware that there is no cheese in this sandwich, even though it's in the Cheese section of the book. But after you taste it, we can promise you'll forget about whatever nitpicky complaints you had about miscategorization. This is really all about the mayo, which is a bit of a game changer.

If you're not hip to the homemade mayo game, it's a popular misconception that emulsification requires egg yolks. Once, when visiting the Institute of Culinary Education (ICE) while Jamie was teaching there, the famous molecular gastronomist Hervé This told the students that he could (though, he insisted, he never *would*) make an emulsion from his spit! He explained that all that is required to create an emulsion such as mayonnaise is water and protein—both readily available in human saliva.

The next day, Jamie went into the kitchen at ICE and made carrot "mayonnaise" with his students by emulsifying oil into a mixture of egg white powder and carrot juice. It worked, and was delicious. As they tasted and discussed, a student suggested making it again with tomato—*to-mayo,* if you will. And Jamie immediately knew where this to-mayo should go: on a BLT! After all, a great BLT begins with good bread and mayo, so why not get the tomato into that mix?

MAKES
4 sandwiches

COMPOUND
geranylacetone

AROMAS
green, hay, magnolia

8 slices thick-cut bacon FAT, SALT, UMAMI

8 slices good-quality bread

¼ cup To-Mayo (recipe follows) FAT, UMAMI

8 slices beefsteak tomato, room temperature UMAMI

Salt SALT

Freshly ground black pepper SPICY

4 to 8 leaves crisp lettuce

Cook the bacon slices in a large sauté pan or cast-iron skillet over medium heat to the desired doneness (chewy or extra-crispy, we won't judge). Transfer the bacon to paper towels to drain and rest. Leave about 1 tablespoon of the bacon fat in the pan. Add the bread to the pan and toast each slice on one side.

To assemble the sandwiches, spread the untoasted side of the bread slices with To-mayo. Arrange the bacon on top of the To-mayo on the bottom slice of bread, add a layer of tomato

continued

slices, and season lightly with salt and pepper. Place the lettuce on top of the tomatoes, then top with the other piece of bread, To-mayo side down. Serve immediately.

TO-MAYO

1 tablespoon tomato paste
UMAMI

½ teaspoon sherry vinegar
SOUR

1½ teaspoons soy sauce SALT, UMAMI

2 tablespoons aquafaba, 1 teaspoon egg white powder, or 1 fresh large egg white

1 cup canola oil FAT

Combine the tomato paste, vinegar, soy sauce, and aquafaba or egg white powder in a small bowl and whisk until thoroughly combined and foamy.

Gradually add the canola oil, pouring in a steady stream while whisking vigorously, until the all oil had been added and the mixture is emulsified. Store in the refrigerator in an airtight container for up to 2 weeks.

Aquafaba, the liquid from canned chickpeas, is a fantastic vegan substitute for egg whites. It can be whipped to fluffy peaks or used as an emulsifier as in this recipe. If you don't care whether the mayo is vegan, you can use egg white powder, which also acts as an emulsifier without adding any extra liquid, which can cause the mayo to be a bit thin. If you do not have egg white powder, a fresh egg white is also fine.

MAKES
about 1 cup

FRICO, AKA CRISPY CHEESE CAKES

broccoli rabe, cheese, onion

We love making roasted broccoli sprinkled with parmesan cheese. Inevitably, when it comes out of the oven, we fight over the crispy bits of parmesan that are left baked onto the pan, known in Italian as *frico.* Then it hit us: Why fight over those little bits when we can make an entire dish that is just one giant crispy piece of cheese with delicious vegetables tucked inside?

SERVES 4 as a
side or appetizer

COMPOUND
2-butenal

AROMA
pungent

**1 russet potato (about
8 ounces)**

Kosher salt SALT

**1 bunch broccoli rabe, stem
ends trimmed by 1½ inches**
BITTER

1 tablespoon olive oil FAT

**1 cup sliced onion (about
1 medium onion)**

3 cloves garlic, thinly sliced
UMAMI

**12 ounces white cheddar
cheese, grated (about 3 cups)**
FAT, SALT, UMAMI

**4 ounces parmesan cheese,
grated (about 1 cup)** FAT, SALT,
UMAMI

Peel the potato and slice into rounds about ½ inch thick. Place the potato slices in a saucepot and add enough cold water to cover by 3 to 4 inches. Season well with salt. Bring to a boil, then reduce the heat to simmer. Cook until the potato is just tender throughout, about 6 minutes after coming to a boil.

Carefully lift the potato slices from the simmering water with a slotted spoon and place them on a plate to steam-dry, leaving the simmering water on the stove.

Drop the broccoli rabe into the simmering water and cook for about 2 minutes, until the stems are just tender, with a slight resistance when pierced with the tip of a knife. Drain and spread into a single layer on a separate plate to steam-dry. When cool enough to handle, chop into ½-inch pieces.

Heat the olive oil in a 10-inch nonstick sauté pan over medium-high heat. Add the onions and sauté for about 2 minutes, until softened, then add the garlic and cook for about 2 minutes more, until aromatic and lightly browned. Slide the onions and garlic onto the plate with the potatoes and return the pan to the heat.

Be careful not to overcook the potato here; if the water is boiling too rapidly or if it cooks for too long, it will turn into a crumbly mess.

continued

Combine the cheddar and parmesan. Scatter half of the cheese mixture in the pan and spread it into an even layer with a heatproof spatula. Reduce the heat to medium and let the cheese cook undisturbed.

When the cheese is completely melted, begins to look a little greasy, and has lightly browned at the edges, scatter half of the potato and onion mixture over the cheese, then add half of the chopped broccoli rabe on top of that. Gently spread and press the vegetables into the cheese. At this point, the cheese should be one solid disk that is well browned on the pan side and soft and creamy on the vegetable side.

Remove the pan from the heat. Carefully slide a heatproof spatula under one side of the cheese and in one quick motion, fold it in half, like an omelet. Slide the folded frico onto a plate to cool before slicing.

Repeat with the remaining cheese, potatoes, onion, and broccoli rabe.

Serve sliced into wedges, slightly warm or room temperature.

Give the pan an occasional gentle swirl to ensure the cheese is not sticking.

LAND

Chicken

Chicken makes frequent and recurring appearances on our dinner table, and our lunch plates, too, for that matter. A generally lean protein with mild flavor, it is exceptional at taking on other flavors, blending seamlessly into nearly any cuisine or cooking style. We don't like to tie specific cuts of chicken to any one recipe or preparation. There are cuts we prefer for some recipes, but truly any cut of chicken (or other variety of poultry) can be used in any recipe. Cooking chicken is all about the time/temperature relationship.

Lean cuts from the breast should be cooked just to the point of doneness and no longer. These lean cuts lack the intramuscular fat and connective tissue that help keep dark meat (wings, thighs, and legs) juicy throughout the cooking process. When any piece of meat is cooked, proteins begin to denature as a result of being exposed to heat. Think of this process as if the proteins are individual strands of rope that weave themselves into a net as they are cooked. When meat is cooked properly, this net holds in the majority of the water that muscle fibers naturally contain. The longer the proteins are exposed to heat, the more the net tightens, eventually to a point that all of the water is squeezed out of the net and you are left with dry, tasteless chicken. The problem with chicken is that this net starts to squeeze tight at temperatures that are just beyond what is regarded as safe for consumption (165°F). Cooked chicken will begin to rapidly lose moisture at 175°F, which means there is a very short grace period between cooked and dried out. The best approach when cooking lean cuts of chicken is to cook them to about 155°F, remove them from the pan, grill, oven, or wherever they may be cooking, and place them on a wire rack to rest. As the meat sits on the rack it will continue to cook (its internal temperature will continue to rise) for at least 5 minutes; by the time the temperature stops rising, it should have the reached the 165°F mark. (This is known as carryover cooking.) This is less of a concern with chicken legs, thighs, and wings, as the fat and connective tissue naturally present in the meat will help keep it more tender and moist than lean white meat cuts.

Brines can provide an extra layer of protection from dry, overcooked meats by promoting water retention or actually adding moisture to the meat before it is cooked. A basic brine can be made by combining 2 cups room temperature water, 2 tablespoons kosher salt, and 1 tablespoon sugar in a bowl and whisking until the salt and sugar are dissolved. You can build additional flavor into this basic formula by adding spices or herbs, or changing the sweetener (brown sugar, maple syrup, honey, etc.). Submerge raw chicken in the brine for at least 2 hours, up to overnight. Brining should be done in the refrigerator in a covered container. Remove the chicken from the brine (and discard the brine) when you're ready to cook.

LIGHT OR DARK?

Lean cuts of poultry lend themselves well to high-heat cooking methods in which cooking times are kept short, like grilling, searing/sautéing, and high-temperature roasting—these methods are efficient and provide flavor via the Maillard reaction, a kind of browning.

Maillard browning, which is different from caramelization in that it involves proteins and the breakdown of sugars, is responsible for the distinctive roasted and toasted aromas in a variety of delectable food items, from seared steak to fresh-baked bread and a whole lot in between. The aromas associated with Maillard browning

have been shown to immediately trigger hunger and craving.

As we mentioned, the fat and connective tissue naturally present in poultry legs, thighs, and wings allow the meat to become tender and remain moist through longer cooking times, where you'll want lower cooking temperatures. Barbecue, smoking, slow-roasting, braising, and slow-cooking are ideal methods for these cuts.

THE MYTH OF COOKING ON THE BONE

For ages we've heard the mantra that cooking meats on the bone means more flavor. Here's the problem: Bone imparts no flavor whatsoever to meat while it cooks. Rather, the bones, which contain about 15 percent water, are very poor conductors of heat and slow the cooking process. Because of this, the meat surrounding the bone cooks more slowly and will likely retain more moisture. The slower cooking also means it's also less likely to overcook and become dry, so it's therefore perceived as more flavorful.

Bottom line: Bones make meats cook more *slowly.* Even if you monitor cooking temperatures and are careful not to overcook the meat, bones provide no added benefit to flavor in the cooking process.

WHY DO WE COOK CHICKEN TO **165°F?**

Salmonella, a dangerous bacteria, is killed instantly at 165°F. If the chicken's internal temperature reaches 165°F, there is no possible chance for salmonella infection. This is an especially important consideration when dealing with ground meats, in which bacteria like salmonella could potentially be found anywhere within in the meat. However, when dealing with whole cuts like a chicken breast or thigh, any bacterial contamination would be most likely to occur on the surface. In these cases, surface bacteria will be eliminated during the normal cooking process (grilling, searing, roasting, etc.).

In the following recipes you will see that we advise you cook all chicken to 165°F because we don't want to be responsible for you getting sick. However, at home when we know that we have good, wholesome chicken, we routinely cook chicken breasts to 145° to 150°F. Though the USDA does not regard this temperature as universally safe, the proteins in chicken have gone through the denaturation process (meaning it's cooked) by the time the internal temperature reaches 145°F.

CHICKEN COOKING TEMPERATURE LINE

175°F Overcooked. Lean proteins begin to rapidly lose moisture and become dry.

165°F Safe Temperature. Salmonella and other bacteria are instantly killed at this temperature.

145°F Proteins are denatured (aka cooked). At this temperature, the proteins in chicken have nearly completed the denaturation process and the meat will have a firm, cooked texture.

135°F* Connective tissue begins to break down and tougher cuts like legs, wings, and thighs will become tender over time if held at or above this temperature.

*Not safe to eat at this temperature

40°F Storage, Raw. Chicken should be kept at or below 40°F before cooking.

SPICY POMEGRANATE AND CHICKEN LETTUCE WRAPS

chicken, pomegranate, chile, lemongrass

Sometimes dinner just needs to be quick and easy, and that's exactly what this recipe is. It's ready in about 15 minutes, but the best part is that it is as good the next day for lunch as the day you make it. This craveable combination is based on the strong citrus aromas that link together pomegranates, chile, and lemongrass. It's an apt match and chicken is happy to come along for the ride.

SERVES 4 to 6

COMPOUND
2-ethyl-1-hexanol

AROMAS
citrus, green, oil, rose

2 tablespoons sesame oil FAT, UMAMI

Two 3-inch pieces lemongrass stalk, crushed (optional)

1 tablespoon minced garlic UMAMI

1 tablespoon minced fresh peeled ginger SPICY

2 tablespoons thinly sliced scallion (green and white parts)

1 jalapeño chile, seeded and minced SPICY

Fresh lemongrass adds incredible flavor and brightness to this (or any) recipe. Lemongrass is all about aroma, as the stalks are very tough and fibrous, making them quite unpleasant to eat. Crushing the lemongrass by beating it with the back of your knife releases the maximum aroma from the stalk.

1 pound ground chicken UMAMI

4 fresh lime leaves (optional)

1 teaspoon cornstarch or rice flour

2 tablespoons soy sauce SALT, UMAMI

1 cup pomegranate juice BITTER, SWEET

1 tablespoon toasted sesame seeds

1 tablespoon packed fresh mint leaves

1 tablespoon packed fresh cilantro leaves

½ head iceberg lettuce, leaves separated, for serving

Heat the oil in a large sauté pan or wok over high heat, and add the lemongrass, if using. When the lemongrass begins to sizzle, stir in the garlic, ginger, scallion, and jalapeño. Stir-fry until aromatic, about 20 seconds. Add the chicken and lime leaves, if using. Immediately break the chicken up into pieces. Continue cooking until the chicken is fully cooked and any juices that accumulated in the pan are completely dry, 6 to 8 minutes more. Scatter the cornstarch over the chicken and stir until absorbed.

Deglaze the pan with the soy sauce and stir until nearly dry. Add the pomegranate juice and cook, stirring constantly, until the juice is thickened and slightly syrupy, 2 to 3 minutes. Transfer to a plate and garnish the chicken with the sesame seeds, mint, and cilantro. Serve with lettuce leaves to make wraps.

PAN-ROASTED CHICKEN WITH CREAMED GREENS AND POTATOES

chicken, mustard greens, cream, lemon

Once your ingredients are prepared, this one-pan roast is ready in 30 minutes. If you make it with chicken breasts instead of thighs, cut the cooking time in half. The flavors focus on pungency and their balancing tastes—cumin and mustard greens are pungent, lemon and sour cream create balance.

SERVES 4

COMPOUND
leaf aldehyde

AROMAS
almond, fat, green apple, grass

1 tablespoon vegetable oil FAT

1½ pounds boneless chicken (about 6 thighs or 4 breasts) UMAMI

Kosher salt SALT

Freshly ground black pepper SPICY

1 tablespoon unsalted butter FAT

4 cloves garlic, peeled and smashed UMAMI

2 branches fresh thyme

1 teaspoon cumin seeds or ½ teaspoon ground cumin

8 ounces fingerling potatoes, halved lengthwise UMAMI

2 cups chopped mustard greens or kale BITTER

1½ cups chicken stock UMAMI

2 tablespoons sour cream FAT, SOUR

Juice of ½ lemon SOUR

Preheat the oven to 375°F.

Heat the oil in a large oven-safe sauté pan over medium-high heat. While the oil heats, lay the chicken out on a plate and season it well on both sides with salt and pepper.

Pat the skin side of the chicken dry. Transfer the chicken to the hot pan with tongs, placing each piece skin side down. Reduce the heat to medium and leave the chicken to cook undisturbed for 3 to 4 minutes. Check to see that the chicken is well browned; if it isn't, continue cooking until it is, another minute or two. Transfer the chicken to a baking pan or clean plate.

Drain any fat from the pan and return the pan to the heat. Immediately add the butter, garlic, thyme, and cumin. When the butter has melted, add the potatoes and toss to coat them. Season with salt and pepper and return the chicken to the pan, skin side up.

Transfer the pan to the oven and roast for 12 to 14 minutes for boneless beasts or about 25 minutes for boneless thighs, until a thermometer inserted into the thickest part reads 160°F.

After coming out of the oven, the chicken will reach at least 165°F due to carry-over cooking.

continued

When the chicken is finished cooking, remove it from the pan to rest on a wire rack or a clean plate and set the pan back on the stove over medium-low heat. Cook for 2 to 3 minutes, stirring often, so that the fat remaining in the pan begins to sizzle and turns clear (not colorless).

Add the mustard greens to the pan and sauté until just wilted, about 1 minute. Deglaze the pan with the chicken stock and cook until the liquid is reduced by three-quarters, 4 to 6 minutes.

Remove the pan from the heat, stir in the sour cream and lemon juice, then return the chicken to the pan and toss to coat. Serve immediately.

This process of "clarifying" the fat is basic technique for making a pan gravy. By simmering the pan drippings, the juices that came out of the chicken during cooking reduce and turn into a fond that clings to the bottom of the pan, which will then be released in the sauce.

PAN-SEARED CHICKEN WITH HERBED CARROTS AND MUSTARD

dill, butter, lemon, carrot

Think of this as chicken piccata's sweet, saucy cousin. Carrots, dill, and lemon go together incredibly well thanks to the underlying woody and resinous aromas that all three contain (alpha-pinene and alpha-terpinolene). They are very similar to—and friendly with—citrus aromas. It's all the flavors of piccata without the pucker: Carrots lend sweetness and crunch that the original lacks.

SERVES 4

COMPOUND
alpha-terpinolene

AROMAS
pine, plastic, sweet

2 pounds chicken breast cutlets or boneless, skinless thighs UMAMI

Kosher salt SALT

Freshly ground black pepper SPICY

2 tablespoons olive oil FAT

2 tablespoons thinly sliced scallion (green and white parts)

2 cups peeled and sliced carrots (about 2 medium carrots) SWEET

Grated zest and juice of 1 lemon SOUR

4 tablespoons (½ stick) unsalted butter, cut into pieces FAT

1 teaspoon Dijon mustard SPICY

1 tablespoon chopped fresh dill or 1 teaspoon dried dill

Season the chicken with salt and pepper and set aside on a plate.

Heat the olive oil in a large sauté pan over high heat. When the oil begins to shimmer and lightly smoke at the edge, pat the chicken dry and add to the pan. Reduce the heat to medium and cook until well browned on the bottom, about 3 minutes. Flip the chicken and brown well on the second side, about 3 minutes more. Remove the chicken from the pan and let cool on a wire rack.

Drain any excess oil from the pan and add the scallion. Sauté briefly until aromatic but not browned, 30 to 60 seconds. Stir in the carrots and continue cooking until they are just tender, 2 to 3 minutes.

Add the lemon zest and juice to the pan and bring to a bare simmer. Immediately remove the pan from the heat and stir in the butter. Stir constantly until all the butter is melted and incorporated into the sauce. Stir in the mustard and dill and return the chicken to the pan. Turn the chicken to coat with the sauce and serve immediately.

ULTIMATE HONEY-MUSTARD CHICKEN

yogurt, mustard, basil, honey

This is honey-mustard chicken with the flavor turned up to 11. Short and simple, this is the best grilling or broiling marinade you'll ever use. But don't stop at the grill—this marinade makes amazing fried chicken, too! After marinating the chicken, wipe off the excess marinade and dredge the chicken in flour, then dip in beaten eggs and coat with breadcrumbs before pan-frying.

SERVES 4

COMPOUND
2-phenylethanol

AROMAS
fruit, lilac, rose, wine

¼ cup plain yogurt FAT, SOUR

2 tablespoons chopped fresh basil leaves

1 tablespoon Dijon mustard SPICY

1 tablespoon honey SWEET

1 teaspoon kosher salt, plus more as needed SALT

Few dashes Worcestershire sauce UMAMI

1½ pounds boneless chicken (about 6 thighs or 4 breasts) UMAMI

Kosher salt SALT

2 teaspoons smoked paprika

Combine the yogurt, basil, mustard, honey, salt, and Worcestershire in a large bowl or other container suitable for marinating. Whisk until smooth.

Add the chicken to the marinade and turn to coat evenly. Cover the container or transfer the chicken and marinade to a zip-top plastic bag, squeeze out all the air, and seal. Refrigerate the chicken in the marinade overnight, or for up to 48 hours.

To cook, heat a grill to medium and oil the grates, or preheat the broiler. Remove the chicken from the container and wipe off any excess marinade. Season the pieces lightly on both sides with salt and the paprika.

Transfer the chicken immediately to the grill or place on a wire rack on a baking sheet under the broiler. For boneless breasts, cook for about 6 minutes per side; for boneless thighs, cook for about 8 minutes per side. Flip once half way through the cooking, or as needed to prevent the chicken from becoming too dark on either side.

If too much marinade is left on the chicken, it can burn or cause the chicken or stick to the grill.

SOUTHWESTERN GRILLED CHICKEN SALAD

grapes, corn, tomato, cilantro

This recipe gives you fruit aromas from all corners of the produce section without being "fruity." Use any type of cooked chicken you like. If you're firing up the grill for the corn, grilled chicken, such as the Ultimate Honey-Mustard Chicken on page 101, is ideal, but a store-bought rotisserie chicken will do just fine.

SERVES 4

COMPOUND
4-hydroxynonanoic acid lactone

AROMAS
apricot, cocoa, coconut, peach, sweet

2 ears fresh corn, shucked
SWEET

1 tablespoon vegetable oil

Kosher salt SALT

Freshly ground black pepper
SPICY

1 tablespoon apple cider vinegar SOUR

1 teaspoon soy sauce SALT, UMAMI

1 teaspoon sriracha SPICY

1 bunch scallions (light green and white parts only), thinly sliced

1 cup halved grape tomatoes
SWEET, UMAMI

1 cup halved seedless green or red grapes SWEET

2 tablespoons chopped fresh cilantro leaves

1 cup crumbled feta cheese FAT, SALT, SOUR, UMAMI

2 tablespoons olive oil FAT

2 pounds skinless, boneless cooked chicken, shredded or chopped (about 4 cups) UMAMI

Heat a grill to hot and oil the grates, or preheat the broiler.

Lightly coat the corn with the oil and season with salt and pepper. Cook on the grill or underneath a broiler until lightly charred on all sides, 3 to 4 minutes per side. Set aside until cool enough to handle. Shave the kernels off the cob with a sharp chef's knife.

In a large bowl, combine the vinegar, soy sauce, sriracha, and scallions. Mix well. Add the tomatoes, grapes, corn kernels, cilantro, feta, olive oil, and chicken and toss well to combine.

Taste for seasoning, adding salt and more sriracha as needed. The flavor of the salad will improve for a few hours after mixing, but will begin to decline after 24 to 36 hours as the grapes and tomatoes begin to break down and become watery. If you need to prepare this in advance, it is best to cook the corn and make the dressing in advance, then keep all the ingredients separate and mix everything together 2 to 3 hours before serving.

If you're not a fan of cilantro, it's okay—it's your parents' fault, not yours. Most people who strongly dislike cilantro have a genetically determined aroma receptor that experiences cilantro as a soapy flavor. You can substitute fresh basil.

Working one at a time, stand an ear of corn up in the center of your cutting board, or in a bowl to contain the kernels. Carefully cut down the length of the cob to separate the kernels from the cob. Cut one straight row down the length of the cob, then rotate the cob and repeat. Continue until all of the kernels are off of the cob. Save the cobs for vegetable stock, or discard.

CREAMY TOMATO CHICKEN RAGU

tomato, cream, onion, vodka

Again with the fruit aromas that pair with chicken . . . but in a very different way. Here we are accessing the fruity aromas in tomatoes and complementing them with the floral aromas from dairy—which land this recipe in a delicious spot squarely between a Bolognese and a classic tomato vodka sauce. Of course this sauce is perfect for pasta, but no noodles are required. It is equally good with cooked grains, roasted potatoes, or all on its own. Heck, we've even been known to throw it on a bun and dig in Sloppy Joe–style . . . or Sloppy Giuseppe?

SERVES 4

COMPOUND
2-heptanone

AROMAS
bell pepper, blue cheese, fruit, green

2 tablespoons vegetable oil, plus more as needed FAT

1 pound ground chicken or turkey, or 1 pound boneless, skinless chicken thighs, cut into ½-inch cubes UMAMI

Kosher salt SALT

Freshly ground black pepper SPICY

1 yellow onion, grated

1 tablespoon minced garlic UMAMI

½ cup vodka

Heat the oil in a heavy-bottomed, wide saucepot. When the oil is hot, add the chicken and season well with salt and pepper. Cook, stirring occasionally, until the meat is well browned, 8 to 10 minutes.

When all of the liquid has evaporated from the chicken, stir in the onion and garlic. If the pot seems dry before you add the onion, add a little extra oil. Cook until the onion and garlic are completely tender, 4 to 5 minutes. Stir often as the onions cook and scrape the bottom of the pot with a wooden spoon or heatproof spatula to release the fond before it burns.

Slide the pot off of the heat and carefully pour in the vodka. Stir well and slide the pan back onto the heat. Stand back in case the vapors ignite. If they do, don't panic, simply let the alcohol burn off. The flames will last no more than 45 seconds and nothing in the pot will burn or be damaged in that time.

Grating the onion is way easier than mincing, but also will help the onion to break down completely in the recipe, releasing maximum flavor into the dish. The best way to do this is to place your grater inside a bowl, then grate the onion, to ensure you capture all the juice.

Take your time with this step; it is where all of the flavor is developed. First the meat will turn gray, meaning that it is cooked, and will release some liquid. Continue cooking, stirring occasionally, until all of that liquid has evaporated and turned into a flavor-rich fond on the bottom of the pot.

continued

One 28-ounce can chopped tomatoes, with their juice UMAMI

2 tablespoons chopped fresh basil, plus some whole leaves for garnish

1 cup heavy cream FAT

1 pound dried pasta of your choice (optional)

Grated parmesan cheese, for garnish (optional) FAT, SALT, UMAMI

Stir in the tomatoes and 1 tablespoon of the basil. Mix well. Cover the pot and reduce the heat to a simmer. Cook for 15 minutes, stirring occasionally. Remove the lid and cook for 10 minutes more, still stirring occasionally. Stir in the cream and simmer for another 5 minutes or until thickened. Remove from the heat and stir in the remaining 1 tablespoon basil. If not using immediately, let the sauce cool and then store in an airtight container in the refrigerator for up to 1 week.

To serve with pasta, bring a large pot of heavily salted water to a boil. Cook the pasta al dente, according to package instructions. Transfer the pasta to the pot of sauce, incorporating about ½ cup of the pasta cooking water as well. Simmer the pasta and sauce together for 2 minutes, stirring constantly, until creamy and the pasta is well coated. Serve immediately, garnished with cheese and basil (if desired).

GINGER BEER–BATTERED CHICKEN FINGERS

ginger beer, lime, chili powder

We give classic tempura batter a unique twist by making it with ginger beer—an outstanding flavor pairing for chicken—and adding a little lime and chili powder for fried chicken that's surprising, a little spicy, and oh-so-delicious!

SERVES 4 to 6

COMPOUND
1,8-cineol

AROMAS
camphor, cool, eucalyptus, mint

1¼ cups all-purpose flour, plus more as needed

¾ cup cornstarch

1 tablespoon baking powder

1 tablespoon plus 1 teaspoon kosher salt SALT

1 tablespoon chili powder SPICY

1½ cups ginger beer (one 12-ounce bottle), chilled SWEET, SPICY

Ice water (optional)

Canola or peanut oil, for frying FAT

2 pounds boneless, skinless chicken, cut into strips UMAMI

1 cup mayonnaise FAT

Grated zest and juice of 1 lime SOUR

Lime wedges, for garnish SOUR

Combine the flour, cornstarch, baking powder, and 1 teaspoon of the salt in a large bowl. Whisk well to combine. In a separate small bowl, mix the remaining tablespoon salt with the chili powder. Set aside.

Whisk the ginger beer into the flour mixture. It should have the consistency of pancake batter. If the mixture is too thick, add ice water 1 tablespoon at a time to reach the desired consistency.

Pour enough oil into a 6- to 8-quart pot to fill it to a depth of about 3 inches. Heat the oil to 350°F.

While the oil heats, lay the strips of chicken out on a platter or baking sheet and season lightly with the chili-salt mixture. Scatter flour over the chicken and toss to lightly coat.

One at a time, dip the chicken strips into the batter then gently lower into the hot oil. Working in batches, cook until golden brown and crisp, about 6 minutes per batch. Do not crowd the pot. As each piece finishes cooking, transfer it to a wire rack to drain. Season again lightly with the chili-salt mixture.

Mix the mayonnaise with the lime zest, juice, and chili salt to taste to make a dipping sauce. Serve the chicken with the mayo and lime wedges to squeeze on top.

Look for a low-sugar ginger beer. If it is too sweet, the batter will burn before the chicken has finished cooking through. If you can't find a low-sugar option, use 1 cup ginger beer and ½ cup club soda.

Coating the chicken with a small amount of flour will help the batter to stick to the meat. Otherwise the crisp coating will tend to slip or flake off.

INDIAN CHICKEN AND GREEN VEGETABLE PILAU

green peas, cucumber, hazelnuts

Sauvignon blanc typically brings to mind notes of citrus and melon. However, green vegetable—and more specifically green bell pepper—is one of the most important aromas found in the wine. In this easy stir-fry, peas, cucumber, and jalapeño all hit different notes of "green" that complement an accompanying glass of sauvignon blanc perfectly, while crisp acidity in each sip refreshes between spicy bites—although this dish is perfectly delicious even if you're just drinking water.

SERVES 4

COMPOUND
(E)-2-nonenal

AROMAS
cucumber, fat, cut grass, watermelon

2 pounds boneless, skinless chicken breasts UMAMI

2 teaspoons garam masala SPICY

1 teaspoon kosher salt SALT

1 tablespoon ghee or vegetable oil FAT

3 tablespoons unsalted butter FAT

1 cup thinly sliced yellow onion

3 cloves garlic, peeled and smashed UMAMI

3 slices peeled fresh ginger SPICY

1 teaspoon cumin seeds

½ teaspoon ground coriander

1 cup jasmine or basmati rice

2 cups chicken stock

1 cup frozen petit peas or baby sweet peas

2 Kirby cucumbers, thinly sliced

¼ cup toasted hazelnuts or peanuts (see tip, page 21) FAT

½ green jalapeño chile, seeded and sliced SPICY

1 tablespoon fresh lime juice SOUR

2 tablespoons extra-virgin olive oil FAT

2 tablespoons cilantro leaves, for garnish

After toasting the nuts, crush them by placing them on a cutting board and pressing firmly with the bottom of a clean pot

Season the chicken on both sides with the garam masala and salt.

Place a large sauté pan over high heat and add the ghee. When the pan and oil are very hot, add the chicken to the pan, making sure the pieces are in a single layer without touching. Cook in batches if necessary. Cook the chicken until well browned on both sides, 2 to 3 minutes per side. Remove from the heat and let the chicken rest on a wire rack.

Drain any fat from the pan and add the butter. Place the pan back over high heat and add the onions, garlic, and ginger. Cook until tender and lightly browned. Stir in the cumin, coriander, and rice. Sauté for about 1 minute, until very fragrant. Stir in the chicken stock and return the chicken pieces to the pan. Cover with a lid and bring to a simmer. Reduce the heat to low and cook, covered, for about 15 minutes, until the rice has absorbed all the liquid. Remove the pan from the heat, gently stir in the peas, then replace the cover and let stand for 5 minutes.

While the chicken is simmering, combine the cucumbers, hazelnuts, jalapeño, lime juice, and olive oil in a bowl. Mix well and season to taste with salt.

To serve, spoon the chicken and rice onto plates, top with the cucumber salad, and garnish with cilantro.

Beef, Pork, and Lamb

These meats are really far more similar than they are different. All three animals have the same basic bone and muscle structure, and eat very similar diets. Furthermore, the ultimate flavor developed in a cut of meat is largely influenced by its cooking method, as raw meat generally has very little aroma. The flavor in cooked meats mostly comes from the pyrazines and pyridines generated by the Maillard browning (see page 93). There are three main fatty acids that play a role in these aromas, and though they are influenced by genetics, diet is more important.

- Grass-fed animals have higher concentrations of linolenic acid and have a clean, fatty flavor.

- Grain-fed animals develop more oleic and linoleic acid for a fatty, fried flavor.

- Corn-finished animals develop less caproic acid, and have more of a cheesy-fatty flavor.

Aging also plays an important role in the flavor of meat. Beef in particular has very little flavor before aging. A key aromatic in beef and pork flavor, 1-octen-3-ol, can increase tenfold in the first fourteen days of beef aging. The compound (E,E)-2,4-decadienal is created by the oxidation (aging) of linoleic acid and contributes to the unique flavor of lamb.

Retail cuts of meat undergo a minimum of seven days of aging. The vast majority of meat that you find at your local grocery is wet aged. Despite its name, no liquid is added to the meat during this process. In wet aging, the meat is simply vacuum sealed to prevent oxidation and moisture loss as it ages under standard refrigeration. In dry aging, the meat is held in a highly precise environment where temperature, humidity, and even light exposure are carefully controlled. During the dry aging process, the meat will lose moisture, giving it more concentrated flavor. Enzymes also develop in the meat that begin to naturally break down connective tissue within the muscles, making the meat more tender.

There is not one perfect answer for which cut of meat should be used in a particular recipe. With beef, the proper cut is sometimes best chosen by budget and time. A skirt steak is relatively inexpensive, cooks quickly, and is flavorful and tender when sliced. It makes a recipe like Grilled Beef and Eggplant with Espresso Butter (page 119) perfect for a weeknight dinner. However, prepare the same recipe with thick-cut filet mignon and it becomes a stunning special occasion meal. We encourage you to try these recipes, get to know them, then dress them up or down so they're perfect for the meal *you* want that day.

Fat is the key to flavorful meat. It helps keep the meat moist throughout the cooking process. This holds true for beef, pork, and lamb. Highly marbled cuts of meat are the most forgiving to cook and taste better. They also tend to be the most expensive. Leaner cuts, or cuts with more connective tissue—such as stew meat (typically cubes from the shoulder) or shanks—can be a bit more temperamental, but can be equally delicious if cooked well. These cuts can yield deeply flavorful and highly satisfying meals that are sometimes preferable to the more expensive cuts.

How you chose to cook your meat should be largely determined by the cut you select. Cuts from the center part of the animal, between the shoulder blades and the hips, with more marbling and smaller amounts of connective tissue, are the typical "steak" cuts; they are naturally tender and should be cooked quickly, over high heat. They are the cuts best cooked to lower desired temperatures in beef and lamb or to 145°F in pork. Cuts from the shoulder and hind leg have more connective tissue and require longer cooking

and lower heat. As the connective tissue is exposed to heat, it slowly begins to break down and transforms from dense and chewy to tender and creamy. The elastin and collagen in connective tissue become gelatin, giving slow-cooked meats their distinctive, rich mouthfeel. This slow cooking process allows these leaner cuts to become tender and moist; if cooked at high heat, the connective tissue would toughen and the meat dry out.

No matter the cut, salt is the most essential part of the cooking process. As soon as you get your meat home, take it out of its packaging it is in and pat it dry. Lightly salt the meat on all sides, then wrap in butcher paper or loosely cover in a glass or plastic container. This light salting will help to dry the surface of the meat so that when cooked, the meat will more readily develop a brown, seared crust. It will also give the salt time to penetrate the meat, resulting in fuller flavor throughout.

When it comes time to cook, there is no need to remove the meat from the refrigerator for any set time before cooking. It's an enduring myth, but the truth is that setting a steak on a plate on your countertop for 30 minutes before taking it to the grill will have zero net effect on the eventual doneness or its browning.

We use a variety of cooking techniques for different cuts of meat. Don't feel bound to replicate the recipes exactly. Try the beef recipes with lamb or the pork recipes with beef. Use the information on these pages to guide you—then cook what you like.

GENERAL TEMPERATURES FOR DONENESS OF RED MEATS

Rare
120–130°F

Medium-rare
130–135°F

Medium
135–145°F

Medium-well
145–155°F

Well done
155°F and above

SLOW COOKER SWEET POTATO AND ALE BEEF STEW

sage, sweet potato, beer

Limonene, as its name would suggest, is the most prominent compound in the aroma of all citrus fruits. But it's present in other foods, too, and in this recipe, we pull together citrus-adjacent ingredients without using any actual citrus. Beer and sage in particular add bright flavors to this hearty and crowd-pleasing stew.

SERVES 4 to 6

COMPOUND
limonene

AROMAS
balsamic, citrus, fragrant, fruit, greenery, herb

2 pounds beef chuck cubes
UMAMI

1 tablespoon kosher salt SALT

1 teaspoon freshly ground black pepper SPICY

1 teaspoon smoked paprika

¼ teaspoon ground cumin, plus more for serving

2 tablespoons all-purpose flour, or a gluten-free alternative

2 tablespoons vegetable oil

1 medium onion, thinly sliced

1 head garlic, with top cut

Yup, the whole thing, as you would for preparing roasted garlic (see page 43)

Place the beef cubes in a bowl and add the salt, pepper, paprika, and cumin. Toss well to combine. Add the flour and toss again to coat.

Heat the vegetable oil in a large cast-iron skillet or nonstick sauté pan over high heat. When the oil is hot, add the beef cubes so the pan is full but none of the pieces are touching one another. Cook, flipping the cubes, until the beef is browned evenly on all sides, 3 to 4 minutes for each side.

As the beef cubes brown, transfer them to a slow cooker. When all the beef has browned, add the onion and garlic to the pan and sauté for about 2 minutes, until aromatic and lightly browned at the edges, then transfer the onions and garlic to slow cooker as well.

Overcrowding the pan will prevent the beef from browning properly; work in batches if necessary.

One 12-ounce bottle ale-style beer BITTER

4 branches fresh sage or 1 tablespoon dry sage

2 sweet potatoes (about 1 pound), peeled and cut into 2-inch cubes SWEET

1 tablespoon extra-virgin olive oil FAT

Toasted bread, for serving

½ cup sour cream FAT, SOUR

Baguette slices would do, but rye or pumpernickel toast cut into pieces would be an ideal match here.

Pour the beer into the slow cooker and add the sage. Cook on low for 8 hours or high for 4 hours. Add the sweet potatoes halfway through the cooking time.

Remove the garlic from the cooker and set it aside to cool. When the garlic is cool enough to handle, squeeze the whole head from the root end over a bowl. The creamy cooked cloves of garlic will pop out into the bowl. Add the olive oil to the garlic and mash with a fork until a rough paste forms.

Spread the garlic paste on the toasted bread. Serve each bowl of stew with a spoonful of sour cream, a pinch of cumin, and some garlic toast.

You can add the sweet potatoes earlier if you must for convenience, but they may turn out a little mushy.

PAN-SEARED BEEF WITH BOURBON-RAISIN SAUCE

raisins, bourbon, mustard, worcestershire

In this recipe, the savory-sweet combo of roasted meat and bourbon-soaked raisins takes center stage. The success of this dish comes down to kitchen fundamentals. A deep brown sear on the meat creates abundant savory aromas via the Maillard reaction, which are essential to balance the sweet notes coming from the raisins and bourbon. If you find the sauce too sweet for your taste, add a few drops of red wine vinegar or sherry vinegar at the end to balance it.

SERVES 4

COMPOUND
2,4,5-trimethyloxazole

AROMAS
nut, sweet

One 2-pound piece beef tenderloin or strip loin, trimmed and tied UMAMI

Kosher salt SALT

Freshly ground black pepper SPICY

2 tablespoons canola oil FAT

4 tablespoons (½ stick) unsalted butter FAT

4 cloves garlic, peeled and smashed UMAMI

4 to 6 branches fresh thyme

3 or 4 branches fresh rosemary

½ cup bourbon SWEET

¼ cup raisins SWEET

1 cup chicken stock

2 tablespoons Dijon mustard SPICY

3 dashes of Worcestershire sauce UMAMI

Pat the roast dry and season well with salt and pepper.

Preheat the oven to 425°F.

Before cooking, pat any excess moisture off the meat. Place a large oven-safe sauté pan or cast-iron skillet over high heat. Add the oil and heat until the oil begins to smoke. Add the roast and brown well on all four sides, 3 to 4 minutes per side.

Remove the meat from the pan and drain any excess fat from the pan. Add 2 tablespoons of the butter, the garlic, thyme, and rosemary. Return the meat to the pan. As the butter melts and the herbs sizzle, spoon the melted butter over the roast repeatedly to baste it, for 2 to 3 minutes.

When cooking a larger roast like this, if you are not able to pre-salt the meat (see page 111), it is essential to let the seasoned meat sit for 30 minutes to 1 hour before cooking. It is best to season the meat 24 hours or more before cooking. (Refrigerate the meat if it will be sitting for longer than 90 minutes; less than that and room temperature is fine.) This time allows the salt to penetrate the meat and draw out excess moisture and helps concentrate the flavor of the meat.

Transfer the pan to the oven and roast until the meat reaches an internal temperature of 130°F for medium-rare. Remove the meat from the pan and place it on a wire rack to rest while you prepare the sauce.

Discard the garlic and herbs and drain the excess fat from the pan. Place the pan back on the stovetop with the heat off. Pour in the bourbon and raisins and stir well. The pan should sizzle immediately. When the bubbling subsides, turn on the heat to medium and reduce the bourbon by three-quarters, about 1 minute.

Add the chicken stock and cook until it is reduced by about three-quarters, 3 to 4 minutes. Remove the pan from the heat and add the mustard, the remaining 2 tablespoons butter, and the Worcestershire. Stir until the butter has melted and the sauce is emulsified. Transfer the meat to a cutting board and slice against the grain into pieces no thicker than ½ inch. Transfer the sliced meat to a platter to serve. Spoon the sauce over the meat and serve immediately.

Be careful, the bourbon may still ignite! If it does, just step back let it burn out—the flames should only last for 30 seconds at most.

A number of factors will affect how quickly the meat cooks, including the temperatures of your pan and oven, the diameter of the roast, the fat and moisture content of meat, and more. Therefore the exact time in the oven is difficult to predict. It is best to err on the safe side and check the internal temperature after 6 minutes in the oven, then recheck every 6 to 8 minutes after. As the meat gets closer to desired doneness, check the temperature more often.

Keep in mind that the temperature of a roast will rise by 5° to 10°F after it is removed from the oven. So if your desired internal temperature is 125°F, remove the roast from the oven when it is between 115° and 120°F.

SEARED STEAKS WITH ALMOND-CHERRY PESTO

almonds, garlic, oregano, cherry

This is an Italian spin on a unique combination of ingredients—incorporating cherries into a Sicilian-style almond pesto from the city of Trapani. Almonds and cherry are an off-the-charts pairing—botanically, the plants are nearly identical. The compound benzaldehyde creates the distinctive aroma of almonds—in fact, imitation almond flavoring is just a diluted benzaldehyde solution—and also carries strong aromas of cherry fruit. The fruity aromas of both also pair beautifully with beef.

SERVES 4

COMPOUND
benzaldehyde

AROMAS
bitter almond, burnt sugar, cherry, malt

---

2 pounds hanger, flat iron, or skirt steak, trimmed UMAMI

Kosher salt SALT

Freshly ground black pepper SPICY

1 tablespoon vegetable oil FAT

2 tablespoons unsalted butter FAT

2 cloves garlic, peeled and smashed UMAMI

¹⁄₂ cup Almond-Cherry Pesto, for serving (recipe follows)

Lay the steaks out on a platter and season on all sides with salt and pepper. Let rest for 15 to 30 minutes before cooking.

Heat the oil in a large cast-iron skillet or heavy-bottomed sauté pan over high heat. Pat the steaks dry and carefully place them in the pan, working in batches if necessary to avoid overcrowding.

Sear the steaks on one side for 3 to 4 minutes for hanger and flat iron, 1¹⁄₂ to 2 minutes for skirt steak, until well browned. Flip the steaks and add the butter and garlic. Cook until the steaks are browned on the second side, basting as they cook, about 3 minutes, or 1¹⁄₂ minutes for skirt steak. Flip the steaks again, back to the first side, and cook, basting, for 1 minute more, 30 seconds for skirt steak. Remove the steaks from the pan and place on a wire rack to rest.

After the steaks have rested for at least 3 minutes, transfer them to a cutting board. Cut the steaks against the grain into thin slices. Serve with the pesto.

Resting is an important step for cooked proteins. It allows the muscle fibers to relax and hold more of the juices inside. This is particularly important for the cuts in this recipe as they will be sliced before serving. If they are not rested properly, all the juices from the steak will be left behind on your cutting board.

continued

ALMOND-CHERRY PESTO

½ cup red wine vinegar SOUR

½ cup dried sweet cherries
SWEET

1 teaspoon dried oregano

1 cup toasted almonds FAT

1 clove garlic, peeled UMAMI

¼ cup grated pecorino or
parmesan cheese FAT, SALT,
UMAMI

½ cup extra-virgin olive oil,
plus more as needed FAT

Kosher salt SALT

Freshly ground black pepper
SPICY

Combine ½ cup water and the vinegar in a small saucepot
and bring to a boil. As soon as the liquid reaches a boil, add
the cherries and oregano. Reduce the heat to a simmer and
cook until only 1 to 2 tablespoons liquid remain, 4 to 6 minutes.
Remove the pot from heat and set aside to cool slightly.

While the cherries cool, combine the almonds, garlic, and
pecorino in a food processor and blend until they form a paste.

Add the cherries, any juices that remain in the pot, and the olive
oil. Blend again to form a medium paste. Add more olive oil if the
mixture is too thick. Season to taste with salt and pepper. Store
in an airtight container in the refrigerator for up to 10 days.

MAKES 2 cups

GRILLED BEEF AND EGGPLANT WITH ESPRESSO BUTTER

beef, eggplant, espresso

Beef and eggplant are two ingredients that absolutely *love* the flavor of char. In this recipe, we use espresso powder like a megaphone to blast those roasted and charred aromas throughout the dish. Compound butters are a cook's secret weapon—they are the most effective way to add lots of big flavor to a dish with very little effort. You can make them, then wrap tightly and store in the freezer for months, to use whenever you want—which is why the recipe makes more than you'll need. Surprisingly, the same charred aromas that make this dish so craveable link to citrusy aromas like linalool that also make your finished plate bright and fresh.

SERVES 4

COMPOUND
linalool

AROMAS
bergamot, citrus, cilantro, lavender, lemon, rose

4 Japanese eggplant BITTER

Kosher salt SALT

Four 8- to 12-ounce steaks of your choice UMAMI

Freshly ground black pepper SPICY

6 tablespoons Espresso Butter (recipe follows)

4 tablespoons extra-virgin olive oil FAT

2 Kirby cucumbers, sliced (about 1½ cups)

2 teaspoons fresh lemon juice SOUR

¼ cup fresh mint leaves, for garnish

Split the eggplant in half lengthwise.

Lightly score the flesh side of the eggplant with a paring knife to create a diamond pattern. Season the flesh side lightly with salt and let stand while the steaks cook.

Heat a grill to high and oil the grates. Season the steaks well with salt and pepper. Cook to your desired doneness: for thinner steaks like flank or skirt fillet, about 5 minutes per side; for thicker steaks like hanger, rib-eye, or strip, 6 to 8 minutes per side for medium-rare. Lift and rotate the steaks 90 degrees once when cooking each side. Remove the steaks from the grill, place them on a wire rack set over a baking sheet to rest, and top each with 1 tablespoon of the espresso butter. The butter should melt and run over the steaks as they rest.

Pat the eggplant dry and brush the flesh of the eggplant with a generous amount of the olive oil, about 2 tablespoons total.

continued

If they have a large curve or bend, cut each eggplant crosswise into 2 pieces to make splitting them easier.

This will help to draw some of the excess moisture out of the eggplant before cooking.

Season again lightly with salt and pepper. Place the eggplant on the grill, flesh side down. Cook for about 3 minutes, until the edges begin to char and turn black. Flip the eggplant and cook for about 3 minutes on the skin side. Flip again to finish cooking on the flesh side, about 1 minute more. Transfer the eggplant to the rack with the steaks and immediately spread the flesh side with 2 tablespoons espresso butter. Let stand for about 1 minute.

Toss the cucumbers with the lemon juice and the remaining 2 tablespoons olive oil. Season lightly with salt.

If the steaks have cooled, quickly reheat them on the grill, flashing them on the hottest part of the grill for less than 30 seconds total. Transfer them to a cutting board and cut across the grain into slices. To serve, divide the eggplant pieces between four plates and top each with ½ tablespoon of the espresso butter. Place the sliced steak directly on top of the eggplant. Garnish each plate with cucumbers and mint leaves.

ESPRESSO BUTTER

8 ounces (2 sticks) unsalted butter, softened FAT

Grated zest and juice of ½ lemon SOUR

2 tablespoons espresso powder or ground coffee BITTER

1 tablespoon chopped fresh mint

2 teaspoons kosher salt SALT

½ teaspoon freshly ground black pepper SPICY

Combine the butter, lemon zest and juice, espresso powder, mint, salt, and pepper in a bowl. Mix thoroughly until well combined. Keep at room temperature until you're ready to serve. If you have any left over, scoop the remaining butter onto a piece of parchment paper and roll it into a log. Wrap tightly in plastic wrap and refrigerate or store in the freezer for up to 6 months. Slice it while still cold.

MAKES about 20 tablespoons

CHIANTI-BRAISED BEEF WITH GRITS
red wine, corn, butter

This is the signature dish at our restaurant, Angelena's. Our research for *The Flavor Matrix* showed us that beef, red wine, and corn were a great pairing, but exactly how to pull off that combination eluded us for quite a while. It wasn't until we started thinking "outside the cob" that we found what we were looking for. Corn flavor can be found in places other than the yellow kernels on the cob: here, in creamy, buttery grits.

SERVES 6 or more

COMPOUND
2-phenylethanol

AROMAS
fruit, honey, lilac, rose, wine

4 pounds bone-in beef short ribs, trimmed FAT, UMAMI

Kosher salt SALT

Freshly ground black pepper SPICY

1 teaspoon fennel seeds

2 tablespoons vegetable oil FAT

½ cup chopped carrots, 1-inch pieces

1 medium onion, diced

½ cup chopped celery, 1-inch pieces

6 cloves garlic, peeled UMAMI

4 branches fresh thyme

4 branches fresh sage

3 cups Chianti wine, or other dry red wine ACID

3 cups chicken stock UMAMI

Up to 2 tablespoons butter FAT

Creamy Stone-Ground Grits (recipe follows)

Cut the short ribs into portion-size pieces. If the short ribs are bone in, cut them into sections with one bone each. Season the meat generously with salt and pepper and place in a baking dish in a single layer. Scatter the fennel seeds over the meat, cover, and refrigerate overnight.

Preheat the oven to 325°F.

Place a large, heavy-bottomed sauté pan or Dutch oven over high heat and add the oil. While the oil heats, pat the surface of the short ribs dry and season again lightly with salt. Carefully place the ribs in the hot pan and sear until well browned on all sides, about 4 minutes per side. Work in batches, if necessary, to avoid overcrowding. Set the seared ribs aside in a clean baking dish. Drain any excess fat from the sauté pan and return it to the stovetop over medium heat. Add the carrots, onion, and celery to the pan and season with 1 teaspoon salt. Sauté for about 5 minutes, until tender and lightly browned, then stir in the garlic, thyme, and sage and cook for 1 minute more.

If you don't have the time, let the ribs stand for 1 hour at room temperature.

continued

Deglaze the pan with the wine and cook, stirring occasionally, until the wine is reduced by about three-quarters, 6 minutes. Return the short ribs to the pan along with any juices that may have collected. Pour in the chicken stock and bring to a boil. Cover with a lid or aluminum foil and transfer to the oven to cook for 2 hours.

After 2 hours, remove the pan from the oven, uncover, and let rest on the stovetop for 30 minutes. Transfer the short ribs to a clean baking dish or platter and strain the cooking liquid into a small saucepot. (Discard the solids.) Bring the cooking liquid to a bare simmer and cook for about 15 minutes to reduce. While the liquid is simmering, skim any fat from the surface and discard. If not serving immediately, transfer the short ribs to a storage container. Let the reduced cooking liquid cool, then pour it over the short ribs; cover and store in the refrigerator for up to 5 days.

To serve, place the short ribs in a sauté pan and add the strained braising liquid. Cover the pan and bring to a boil. Uncover, reduce the heat to a simmer, and cook until the liquid is reduced by half, about 12 minutes. (If not serving all the short ribs at one time, place the desired number of portions in the pan and add ½ cup of the braising liquid per portion.)

Remove from the heat and transfer the cooked ribs to plates. Add 1 teaspoon butter per portion. Swirl the butter into the pan until the sauce is emulsified. Serve the ribs on top of the grits, with some of the sauce spooned on top.

As the liquid is reducing, turn the ribs so that they heat evenly, and occasionally baste them with the cooking liquid.

CREAMY STONE-GROUND GRITS

1 teaspoon kosher salt SALT

3 tablespoons unsalted butter FAT

1 cup stone-ground grits

Kernels shaved from 1 ear fresh corn (optional) SWEET

½ cup grated parmesan cheese FAT, SALT, UMAMI

Bring 5 cups water, the salt, and 1 tablespoon of the butter to a boil in a medium saucepot. When the water reaches a boil, remove the pot from the heat and add the grits, whisking vigorously for 10 seconds.

Let the pot stand until loose pieces of husk rise to the top of the water and the grits sink. Using a small fine-meshed strainer, scoop the husks from the surface of the water and discard. Whisk to break up any clumps of grits that may have formed at the bottom. Return the pot to the heat, bring to a boil, then adjust the temperature so the grits cook at simmer. Cook, stirring occasionally, until the grits are thick, creamy, and tender, typically 30 to 40 minutes.

When the grits are done, remove the pot from the heat and whisk in the parmesan, the corn kernels (if using), and the remaining 2 tablespoons butter.

MAKES 4 cups cooked grits

Be sure to taste the grits. Do not judge them only by thickness; sometimes grits will thicken quickly, yet remain tough or "gritty." If this happens, add more water and continue cooking until tender.

Pork

Heritage breeds of pork like Berkshire, Duroc, Spotted Pig, and Mangalitsa grow to maturity more slowly than industrially raised breeds. These pigs require more feed and space to roam, and therefore are more expensive to raise. Though higher priced, heritage breeds of pork yield meat that's much more flavorful, with a higher ratio of fat to lean and a richer coloring (more red than white). Like grass-fed beef, pasture-raised pigs develop high quantities of omega 3-fatty acids and linoleic acid.

When cooking pork, the goal should be to reach an internal temperature of 145°F, according to the USDA. At this temperature the interior of the pork should still have a rosy blush. It is not necessary to cook pork so well done that the interior is completely white and firm. Better farming practices and higher food safety standards have nearly eliminated the risks formerly associated with undercooking. By cooking all of the color out of your pork, the only thing you're eliminating is flavor.

Maillard flavors make the best pairings for pork, especially darker aromas like caramel or roasted. Pork also goes very well with fruity aromas, whether they are found in tropical fruits, chiles, or tomatoes.

GRILLED PORK WITH SPICY PINEAPPLE AND BASIL RELISH

pork, pineapple, basil

This recipe is designed to complement the smoky, rich flavor of grilled pork. Try it with your favorite cut—grilled tenderloin, chops, sausages, or smoked pork shoulder. The relish works really great with chicken and fish, too. Pineapple and basil are the star pairing here; the other ingredients play a supporting role.

SERVES 4

COMPOUND
(Z)-beta-ocimene

AROMAS
citrus, flower, herb, mold, warm spice

½ jalapeño chile, seeded and thinly sliced SPICY

2 tablespoons white wine vinegar SOUR

2 ears fresh corn, shucked SWEET

4 fresh pineapple rings, ½ to 1 inch thick, cored SWEET

3 tablespoons vegetable oil FAT

Kosher salt SALT

2 tablespoons mayonnaise FAT

1 tablespoon soy sauce SALT, UMAMI

1 tablespoon tomato paste UMAMI

Four 6- to 8-ounce boneless pork chops, pork loin slices, or other cut of your choice UMAMI

2 tablespoons chopped basil leaves

Place the jalapeño in a medium bowl and pour the vinegar over. Set aside.

Heat a grill to high on one side and to medium on the other. If using a charcoal grill, do this by piling the coals on one side only; on a gas grill set half the burners to high and the others to medium. Oil the grates.

Lightly coat the corn and pineapple rings with some of the oil and sprinkle with salt. Grill over high heat until lightly charred on all sides, 4 to 6 minutes per side. Transfer to a plate and let cool.

When cool enough to handle, shave the kernels off the cob with a sharp chef's knife (see page 102). Chop the pineapple into ½-inch pieces.

Add the mayonnaise to the jalapeños and mix until smooth. Stir in the soy sauce, tomato paste, corn, and pineapple. Mix well. Set aside until you're ready to serve. You can store the relish in the refrigerator, covered, for up to 2 days.

Season the pork with salt and lightly coat each piece with vegetable oil. Place the pork on the hot side of the grill and cook

continued

for 2 minutes. Lift each piece, rotate it 90 degrees, and place it back on same side of the grill. Cook for an additional 2 minutes, or until well browned on the first side.

Flip the pieces to the second side and place over medium heat. Cook for about 2 minutes. At this point, the pork should be cooked to medium to medium-well, about 140°F. Transfer to a wire rack to rest until the temperature reaches 145°F.

When you're ready to serve, stir the basil into the relish and serve with the pork.

PAN-SEARED PORK MEDALLIONS WITH APPLES, BALSAMIC VINEGAR, AND BOURBON

coffee, balsamic vinegar, apple, bourbon

When we were writing *The Flavor Matrix,* we originally devised this recipe with peaches, and it became a staple in our house. But making it that way in cool fall and winter weather just didn't feel right, so we decided with switch it up with apples and add balsamic vinegar for a little tartness. This remains a ridiculously simple recipe, one that you can pull out whenever you are in a hurry but looking to impress; it packs in unexpected flavors at every step, and it can be on the table in about 20 minutes.

SERVES 4

COMPOUND
4,5-dimethylthiazole

AROMAS
green, nut, roasted, smoke

2 teaspoons kosher salt, plus more as needed SALT

1 teaspoon ground coffee BITTER

1 teaspoon ground coriander

½ teaspoon freshly ground black pepper, plus more as needed SPICY

2 pounds pork tenderloin, trimmed and cut crosswise into 12 medallions UMAMI

2 Golden Delicious apples SWEET

Grated zest and juice of 1 lemon SOUR

4 tablespoons extra-virgin olive oil FAT

2 tablespoons thinly sliced scallion (green and white parts)

Combine the salt, coffee, coriander, and pepper in a small bowl and mix well. Arrange the pork medallions on a plate or baking dish in a single layer and sprinkle the spice mixture evenly on both sides. Set aside to marinate while you prepare the apples.

Peel one apple and cut it into quarters. Cut away the core and cut each piece in half lengthwise to create 8 wedges. Set aside. Leaving the skin on, cut the second apple in half and remove the core. Cut both halves into thin slices and toss with the lemon zest and juice, 2 tablespoons of the olive oil, and the scallions. Mix well to coat and season with a pinch each kosher salt and ground black pepper.

Heat a large cast-iron skillet over medium-high heat. Add 1 tablespoon each of the butter and olive oil. Pat the pork medallions dry with a paper towel and add half of them to the pan in a single layer. Cook, flipping them once, until well browned on both sides, 2 to 3 minutes per side. Transfer them to a wire rack to rest. Discard the fat in the pan, wipe the pan out, and add fresh butter and oil, and cook the remaining medallions.

continued

2 tablespoons unsalted butter
FAT

¼ cup bourbon SWEET

2 tablespoons soy sauce SALT, UMAMI

1 cup chicken stock

2 tablespoons balsamic vinegar SOUR, SWEET

Basil leaves, for garnish (optional)

Although basil is not an herb you would typically think about for a fall/winter flavor profile like this, it is a great pairing with apples and adds a bright, fresh "pop" to the plate.

When all the pork has been cooked, discard all but 1 tablespoon fat from the pan and add the apple wedges. Cook for 2 minutes, stirring well, until lightly browned.

Turn the heat off under the pan. Add the bourbon to the apples and turn the heat back on to medium. Deglaze the pan and reduce the bourbon until the pan is nearly dry. Return all the pork to the pan and add the soy sauce and chicken stock. Simmer for about 2 minutes, then remove from the heat. Divide the pork, cooked apples, and sauce between plates. Top with the sliced apple mixture, drizzle each plate with balsamic vinegar, and garnish with basil (if using).

SLOW COOKER PORK WITH MUSTARD, ORANGE, AND SAGE

mustard, orange, sage

The slow cooker is an awesome tool for convenience, but some slow cooker recipes can be a little "one note" in the flavor department. Not this one! Pork, citrus, and sage are a phenomenal combination. It creates deep and sophisticated flavors that are both comfortable and unexpected. Best of all, it can all happen while you are at work or running weekend errands.

SERVES 6 to 8

COMPOUND
1-heptanol

AROMAS
chemical, green, wood

1 tablespoon plus 1 teaspoon kosher salt SALT

2 tablespoons grainy mustard SPICY

Grated zest of 1 orange

2 teaspoons dried sage

One 3- to 4-pound boneless pork shoulder roast UMAMI

1 yellow onion, thinly sliced

1 tablespoon olive oil FAT

1 tablespoon soy sauce SALT, UMAMI

2 cups chicken stock

Combine the salt, mustard, orange zest, and sage in a small bowl and mix well. Pat the pork shoulder dry and rub on all sides with the mustard mixture, making sure to coat the shoulder completely and use the entire mixture. Place the pork in a baking dish and cover with plastic wrap, or put it in a zip-top plastic bag, squeeze out all the air, and seal. Refrigerate overnight.

Combine the onions, olive oil, and soy sauce in a bowl and toss well to coat. Transfer the onions and liquid to a slow cooker. Set the pork on top of the onions and pour in the chicken stock. Cook for 8 hours on low or 6 hours on high.

Transfer the pork to a cutting board to rest. Pour the onions and juices into a large sauté pan. Bring to a boil, then reduce the heat to a simmer and cook until the liquid is reduced by half, 8 to 10 minutes. As the liquid simmers, skim any fat from the surface.

Slice the pork shoulder, divide between plates, and spoon the onions and reduced cooking liquid over the top.

APPLE-BRINED PORK WITH CARAMELIZED ONION AND BOURBON GRAVY

apple, pork, bourbon, onion

This recipe leans on the fruitier side of the pork and apple pairing, compared to our Pan-Seared Pork Medallions (page 131), which take the same pairing in a more robust setting. Or as Jamie would say in true food chemistry nerd fashion, "This is all about the esters. The fruity aromas in apples are also found in pork, so brining the pork in apple juice just makes it taste . . . pork-ier!" (*Brooke rolls her eyes*) Beyond adding flavor, brining does magical things to pork chops, keeping them tender and juicy throughout the cooking process. Meanwhile, bourbon-creamed onions may very well become one of your favorite toppings for any type of roasted meat. Or potatoes. Ever.

SERVES 4

COMPOUND
2-acetylfuran

AROMAS
balsamic, cocoa, coffee, smoke tobacco

1 cup apple juice SWEET

3 tablespoons soy sauce SALT, UMAMI

1 tablespoon packed brown sugar SWEET

1 tablespoon Dijon mustard ACID

Four 6- to 8-ounce bone-in pork rib chops, or 1½ pounds pork tenderloin UMAMI

1 tablespoon vegetable oil, plus more as needed FAT

1 yellow onion, thinly sliced

¼ cup bourbon SWEET

1 cup heavy cream FAT

2 tablespoons thinly sliced chives

Combine the apple juice, 1 cup water, the soy sauce, brown sugar, and mustard in a bowl and whisk until the sugar is dissolved. Pour into a large zip-top plastic bag, add the pork chops, squeeze out all the air, and seal. Refrigerate overnight or for up to 36 hours.

Place a large sauté pan over high heat. Add just enough oil to coat the bottom of the pan. When the oil is hot and begins to shimmer, add the onions and stir well. Allow the onions to settle and cook for 1 minute without stirring, then mix again. Reduce the heat to medium-low and continue to cook, stirring every 2 to 3 minutes, until they are tender and caramelized, about 30 minutes.

Caramelizing onions is a process that takes some time to do properly. The key is maintaining proper heat throughout. Start the onions on very high heat, then reduce the heat and cook slowly for the remainder. If you notice the onion slices are getting brown at the edges but remaining white in the center, the heat is too high and needs to be reduced.

When the onions are tender through and evenly browned, remove the pan from the heat and add the bourbon. Carefully return the pan to the stovetop and turn the heat to high. Stir well to scrape up any brown bits from the base of the pan. Cook until the bourbon is reduced by half, about 1 minute, then add the cream and cook until the sauce is reduced and thickened, 3 to 4 minutes more. Remove from the heat and stir in the chives. Cover the pan to keep warm while you grill the pork chops.

Heat one side of a grill to high and the other to medium and oil the grates. If using a charcoal grill, do this by piling the coals on one side only; on a gas grill set half the burners to high and the others to medium.

Remove the pork from the brine and pat dry. Discard the brine. Use 1 tablespoon oil to coat the surface of the pork. Place the pork on the hot side of the grill and cook for 2 to 3 minutes. Lift each piece, rotate it 90 degrees, and place it back on the grill on the same side. Cook for an additional 2 to 3 minutes or until well browned on the first side.

Flip the pork to the second side and place over medium heat. Cook for about 5 minutes, then lift, rotate 90 degrees, and cook 5 minutes more. At this point, the pork should be cooked to medium to medium-well, about 140°F degrees (remember that the temperature will continue to rise as it rests and pork tenderloin will require more time)). Transfer to a wire rack to rest until the temperature reaches 145°F.

Serve the pork with the creamy onions.

Setting different temperatures on the grill allows you to cook more evenly, creating hotter areas for browning the exterior and cooler areas for evenly cooking though.

BROWN BUTTER, MAPLE, AND PEAR PORK ROAST

pear, pork, maple

We know that pork chops and apples are classic. But when two ingredients have similar aromatic profiles, they can—and should—be substituted for one another. So it follows that anywhere apples might be used, pears are an easy swap. In this recipe, since pears will tend to become soft with heavy roasting, brown butter and maple syrup are added to boost the roasted aromas without overcooking the fruit.

SERVES 4

COMPOUND
2-pentanone

AROMAS
burnt plastic, ether, fruit

2 pounds pork tenderloin or boneless pork loin, trimmed and cut crosswise into ³/₄-inch-thick medallions UMAMI

2 teaspoons kosher salt, plus more as needed SALT

1 teaspoon ground black pepper

2 Bosc or Anjou pears, slightly firm SWEET

6 tablespoons (³/₄ stick) unsalted butter FAT

2 tablespoons extra-virgin olive oil FAT

2 branches fresh rosemary

1 tablespoon maple syrup, plus more to taste SWEET

Grated zest and juice of 1 lemon SOUR

Arrange the pork medallions on a plate or in a baking dish in a single layer and sprinkle the salt and pepper evenly on both sides. Set aside to marinate while you prepare the pears.

Quarter the pears lengthwise through the core, to make 4 equal wedges. Trim away the core and cut each piece in half lengthwise again to create 8 wedges.

Heat a large cast-iron skillet over medium-high heat. Add 1 tablespoon each of the butter and olive oil along with 1 branch of the rosemary. Pat the pork medallions dry with a paper towel. Cook the pork medallions in two batches, browning them well on both sides, about 2 minutes per side, before transferring them to a wire rack to rest. In between batches, discard the fat in the pan, wipe the pan out, and add fresh butter, oil, and rosemary.

When all the pork has been cooked, remove the pan from the heat and wipe it out. Add the remaining 4 tablespoons butter. Stir the butter constantly as it melts. Return the pan to low heat and continue stirring until the butter stops foaming and takes an amber color. Remove the pan from the heat and continue stirring, watching the color carefully. As soon as the butter turns brown, add the pears and stir well. They may splatter a bit when first added to the pan.

When the pears stop sizzling, return the pan to low heat and cook until the pears are just softened, about 3 minutes. Stir in the maple syrup and lemon zest and juice. Stir well and return the pork to the pan to coat. Serve immediately.

Browning butter can be a bit tricky—one trick is to remove the pan from the heat before the butter is completely browned. The heat in the pan will cause the butter to turn one to two shades darker after being removed from the heat. Adding the pears will stop the browning immediately.

Lamb

You'll find two main styles of lamb on the market, domestic and imported. Domestic lamb, raised in the U.S., tends to be larger and have a milder, sweeter flavor. Imported lamb, mostly raised in Australia and New Zealand, does not grow quite as big, and has a slightly stronger (though not gamy) flavor. The main reason for this difference is the diet of the two animals. Most domestic lamb is grain fed, meaning it will grow more rapidly but will develop less linoleic (fatty) acid than grass-fed lamb. Linoleic acid is the precursor to (E,E)-2,4-decadienal, the compound most responsible for lamb's distinctive flavor. In short, more linoleic acid makes grass-fed lamb taste "lamb-ier."

The process for cooking lamb is identical to that for cooking beef. The main difference is that lamb should not be prepared rare. It is perfectly safe to eat at this temperature—it simply does not taste as good. At rare temperatures (around 120°F), lamb fat will not be completely softened, meaning that it has not released its full flavor and will tend to leave a slick, greasy mouthfeel. Otherwise, feel free to swap beef for lamb and vice versa in any recipe you find in this book.

BRAISED LAMB WITH BLUE CHEESE AND MUSHROOM-POTATO GRATIN

lamb, blue cheese, mushrooms, potato, brandy

"Shepherd's pie" was a dinner of our childhood: ground beef, mashed potatoes, a few veggies, and cheese. It was simple and satisfying—every busy mother's dream. It wasn't until we traveled to Ireland on a "baby-moon" before our son, August, was born that we fell in love with authentic shepherd's pie with tender chunks of lamb that shredded at the touch of a fork. We've taken that memory and kicked it up with some seriously bold flavors from brandy and blue cheese.

SERVES 6 or more

COMPOUND
heptanoic acid

AROMAS
apricot, floral, rancid, sour, sweet

LAMB

2 tablespoons vegetable oil FAT

3 pounds boneless lamb shoulder or leg, cut into cubes UMAMI

2 teaspoons kosher salt SALT

½ teaspoon freshly ground black pepper SPICY

2 cups thinly sliced yellow onion (1 large onion)

8 ounces cremini mushrooms, cleaned and sliced UMAMI

4 cloves garlic, peeled and smashed UMAMI

¾ cup brandy

2 cups chicken stock

4 branches fresh thyme or ½ teaspoon dried thyme

Preheat the oven to 325°F.

Make the lamb: Heat the oil in large, oven-safe sauté pan or Dutch oven over high heat. Season the lamb with the salt and pepper. Add the lamb to the hot oil and cook until well browned on all sides, about 2 minutes per side. When the meat is browned, transfer it to a bowl and set aside to rest.

Add the onions, mushrooms, and garlic to the pan. Sauté over medium heat until tender and lightly browned, 3 to 4 minutes. Return the lamb and any collected juices to the pan and turn the heat to high. Cook until all the juices have evaporated, 4 to 6 minutes more. Remove the pan from the heat and pour in the brandy. Stir well, then carefully return the pan to the heat. Cook until the brandy is reduced by half, 2 to 3 minutes.

Add the chicken stock and thyme and bring to a boil. Taste the liquid for seasoning (it should taste fully seasoned). Cover the pan, transfer to the oven, and cook for 1 hour.

Cook in batches if necessary to give the lamb adequate space to brown. Smaller pieces of meat will release more liquid than a large piece does; if you over-crowd the pan, the meat will not brown properly.

continued

POTATOES

3 cups milk FAT

4 russet potatoes (about 2 pounds), peeled and cut into thin slices UMAMI

1 tablespoon minced garlic UMAMI

1 tablespoon kosher salt SALT

½ cup grated parmesan cheese FAT, SALT, UMAMI

8 tablespoons (1 stick) butter FAT

1½ cups blue cheese crumbles FAT, SALT, UMAMI

Make the potatoes: While the lamb is in the oven, combine the milk, potatoes, garlic, and salt in a large saucepot and bring to a boil. Reduce the heat to a simmer and cook for about 10 minutes, until the potatoes are completely tender—they should be easily crushed with the back of spoon. Remove from the pot from the heat, pour off any excess milk, and reserve. Add the parmesan and butter. Beat the potatoes with an electric mixer until smooth and creamy. Gradually add more milk if necessary to reach the desired consistency. Set aside until the lamb has finished cooking.

After 1 hour, remove the lamb from the oven and raise the oven temperature to 450°F. Uncover the sauté pan and place it on the stovetop over medium heat. Simmer, stirring occasionally, until the liquid in the pan is reduced to a glaze, 12 to 15 minutes.

Transfer the lamb mixture to a large oval or 13 x 9-inch baking dish and spread into an even layer. Spread the potatoes over the lamb mixture. Scatter the blue cheese over the potatoes.Bake until bubbling and browned, 10 to 12 minutes. Let cool for at least 5 minutes before serving.

BRAISED LAMB WITH SPICY PEACH CHUTNEY

corn, peaches, grenache wine

People sometimes take a pass on lamb because they think it's gamy, but fruity aromas (esters and lactones) are surprisingly strong in lamb. In this recipe we bring those flavors to the forefront. Braising is such a great way to cook lamb—the cuts for braising are typically less expensive and the meat transforms to become tender and succulent. We love the bright flavors of grenache wine and peach that make this dish comforting, yet bright and fresh tasting at the same time.

SERVES 4

COMPOUND
(E)-2-nonenal

AROMAS
cucumber, cut grass, fat, paper, watermelon

LAMB

4 lamb shanks (about ¾ to 1 pound each), trimmed UMAMI

Kosher salt SALT

Freshly ground black pepper SPICY

2 tablespoons vegetable oil FAT

1 cup chopped yellow onion (about ½ medium onion)

½ cup chopped celery

½ cup chopped carrots SWEET

1 teaspoon fennel seeds

3 cloves garlic, peeled UMAMI

1 ripe peach, pitted and chopped SWEET

2 cups grenache wine ACID

2 cups chicken stock

2 or 3 branches fresh basil

2 tablespoons unsalted butter FAT

Cook the lamb: Preheat the oven to 350°F. Season the lamb shanks with a generous amount of salt and pepper. Heat the vegetable oil in a Dutch oven over high heat. Add the lamb shanks and brown thoroughly on all sides, about 2 minutes per side. When the lamb shanks are well browned, transfer them to a baking dish and set aside. Drain the fat from the pan.

Return the pan to the stove over medium heat. Add the onions, celery, and carrots. Sauté the vegetables until the onions are slightly softened, about 5 minutes. Add the fennel seeds, garlic, and peach and cook for about 1 minute more.

Deglaze the pan with the grenache wine and return the lamb shanks to the pan. Bring to a boil and cook for 1 minute, then add the chicken stock and basil. Cover the pot and transfer to the oven to cook for 2 hours.

While the lamb cooks, make the chutney: Place a small saucepot over medium heat. Add the mustard seeds and cumin seeds. Toast, swirling the spices in the dry pot; when they begin to crackle and become fragrant, they are ready.

Be careful not to burn the spices, or they will become acrid and bitter.

continued

PEACH CHUTNEY

1 tablespoon yellow mustard seeds SPICY

1 teaspoon cumin seeds

¼ cup red wine vinegar SOUR

1 tablespoon sugar, plus more if needed SWEET

½ teaspoon kosher salt, plus more if needed SALT

1 teaspoon finely grated peeled fresh ginger SPICY

1 jalapeño chile, sliced SPICY

2 firm, underripe peaches, diced SWEET

½ cup grenache wine ACID, BITTER

Creamy Stone-Ground Grits (page 125), for serving

Add 2 tablespoons water, the vinegar, sugar, salt, ginger, and jalapeño and bring to a boil. Stir in the peaches and cook at a simmer until the mixtures thickens and the peaches are tender but not mushy, 4 to 6 minutes.

Adjust the seasoning to taste, adding salt and/or sugar as necessary. Remove from the heat and cool slightly before stirring in the wine. Set aside until you're ready to serve the lamb. The chutney may be made in advance and stored in the refrigerator in an airtight container for up to 2 weeks.

After 2 hours, the lamb should very tender and yield easily when pierced with a fork. Remove the lamb from the oven and transfer the shanks to a plate to rest. Empty the cooking liquid and solids into a bowl, then pour the liquid back into the pot through a fine-mesh strainer. Press lightly on the vegetables and peach in the strainer to extract any remaining liquid, then discard whatever solids remain.

Bring the liquid to a light simmer on the stovetop and skim off any fat that collects on the surface. Simmer to reduce the liquid by half, about 15 minutes. Remove from the heat, whisk in the butter, and return the lamb shanks to the pot. Turn the shanks to coat them well with the sauce. Let sit for at least 5 minutes before serving. If left to cool overnight in the sauce and reheated to serve the next day, the meat will improve even more.

Serve with the peach chutney and grits.

ROAST LAMB AND CARROTS WITH MINT AND LEMON

carrot, mint, lemon, garlic

We live for recipes like this—one simple seasoning that makes two wildly different ingredients taste delicious. Thanks to the compounds shared between lamb, carrots, and mint, prep and cooking is a snap while producing a meal that has some serious wow factor.

SERVES 6 to 8
COMPOUND
heptanoic acid
AROMAS
apricot, floral, sour

2 tablespoons chopped fresh mint, plus whole leaves for garnish

3 tablespoons olive oil FAT

1 tablespoon kosher salt SALT

Grated zest and juice of 1 lemon SOUR

2 cloves garlic, finely grated UMAMI

1 teaspoon smoked paprika

Two 8-rib lamb racks or one 3- to 4-pound boneless lamb leg roast, tied UMAMI

½ pound carrots, cut into pieces 1 inch wide and 2 to 3 inches long SWEET

1 tablespoon vegetable oil FAT

In a small bowl, combine the chopped mint, 2 tablespoons of the olive oil, the salt, lemon zest, garlic, and paprika. Mix well to form a smooth paste.

Place the lamb on a baking sheet, spoon 3 tablespoons of the spice paste over it, and rub to evenly coat all sides. Set the lamb aside for 30 minutes, or cover and refrigerate for up to 24 hours.

Preheat the oven to 425°F.

Place the carrots in a bowl and add 2 tablespoons of the spice paste. Toss to coat. Set aside any remaining spice paste.

Heat the vegetable oil in a large sauté pan. When hot, add the lamb and sear it to brown all sides, 3 to 4 minutes per side.

Transfer the lamb to roasting rack in a roasting pan and rub any remaining spice mixture over it. For medium, roast the lamb racks for 20 to 25 minutes, and the leg for 45 to 50 minutes. A thermometer inserted into the center of thickest part of the roast should read between 125° and 130°F. Transfer to a cutting board and let rest for 10 minutes before slicing.

While the lamb is cooking, spread the seasoned carrots in a single layer on a rimmed baking sheet. Roast until just tender, 15 to 20 minutes. Keep warm while the lamb finishes.

To serve, toss the carrots with the lemon juice, the remaining oil, and mint leaves. Slice the lamb and serve with the carrots.

Though it's conventional wisdom, searing meat before roasting does not lock in the juices. What it does is provide coloring to the outside of the meat that might not otherwise develop during cooking times of 1 hour or less. It also allows more roasted aromas to develop in the meat as it cooks in the oven.

HORSERADISH AND CITRUS–CRUSTED LAMB ROAST

lamb, orange, basil, horseradish

Say it with us: basil equals mint, mint equals basil. Okay, not literally— but their compounds are so similar that they can often be used interchangeably. Here, we are shaking up the tried and true mint-and-lamb combo in favor of basil. But things really get interesting when we pull in some of basil's favorite matches, like orange and horseradish. It all comes together to create one of those "OMG, this is so good, what's in it?" moments. But don't worry, it can be our little secret.

SERVES 6 to 8

COMPOUND
nonanal

AROMAS
citrus, fat, floral, green, soap

Two 8-rib lamb racks or one 3- to 4-pound boneless lamb leg roast, tied UMAMI

Kosher salt SALT

1 tablespoon freshly grated or drained prepared horseradish SPICY

1 tablespoon chopped fresh basil leaves

1 tablespoon extra-virgin olive oil FAT

2 teaspoons Dijon mustard SPICY

1 teaspoon freshly grated orange zest

2 tablespoons vegetable oil FAT

Preheat the oven to 425°F.

Pat the lamb dry and season it with salt on all sides. Set aside for 10 minutes.

In a small bowl, combine the horseradish, basil, olive oil, mustard, and orange zest; mix well.

Dry any moisture that has collected on the surface of the lamb. Heat the vegetable oil in a large sauté pan. Add the lamb and quickly sear it to brown all sides, 3 to 4 minutes per side. Transfer to a roasting rack to rest.

When the lamb is cool enough to handle, rub the horseradish mixture on all sides to evenly coat it. Return the roast to the rack, set the rack in a roasting pan, and transfer to the oven.

For medium, cook the lamb racks for 20 to 25 minutes, and the leg for 45 to 50 minutes. A thermometer inserted into the center of thickest part of the roast should read between 125° and 130°F.

Transfer the lamb to a cutting board and let it rest for 10 minutes before slicing and serving.

If the rub were placed on the meat before searing, the roast would not brown properly and the rub would burn; adding it afterward maximizes flavor.

GRILLED LAMB WITH ANCHOVY VINAIGRETTE

lamb, radish, anchovy, lettuce

This recipe is not for the timid. We are talking about some seriously big flavors here, taking the some of the stronger aromas in lamb and amping them up with even more intense anchovies. The beauty in this is that you make a single mixture that doubles as both marinade and salad dressing.

SERVES 6 to 8

COMPOUND
pyrrolidine

AROMAS
ammonia, fishy

¼ cup red wine vinegar SOUR

3 cloves garlic, minced or finely grated UMAMI

2 anchovy fillets, minced, or 1 teaspoon anchovy paste SALT, UMAMI

½ cup vegetable oil FAT

¼ cup extra-virgin olive oil FAT

3 pounds boneless lamb leg pieces, or 12 to 16 lamb rib or loin chops, trimmed UMAMI

Freshly ground black pepper SPICY

2 heads romaine or 4 heads gem lettuce, chopped

1 cup sliced radishes BITTER, SPICY

½ cup grated parmesan cheese FAT, SALT, UMAMI

Freshly ground black pepper SPICY

Thinly sliced fresh chives, for garnish (optional)

Toasted breadcrumbs or croutons, for garnish (optional)

Combine the vinegar, garlic, and anchovy in a bowl and mix well. Set aside to rest for 5 minutes. Stir in the vegetable and olive oils.

Place the lamb in a zip-top plastic bag and add ¼ cup of the dressing. Squeeze out as much air as possible and seal. Gently massage to evenly coat the lamb. Marinate for 1 hour at room temperature, or up to 48 hours in the refrigerator. Refrigerate the remaining dressing while the meat is marinating.

When you're ready to cook, heat a grill to high on one side and medium on the other (see the grilling instructions on page 127).

Remove the lamb from the bag, wipe off any excess marinade (discard any marinade left in the bag), and season the lamb lightly with pepper. Place the lamb on the hot side of the grill and cook for 2 to 3 minutes, until grill marks appear. Lift the lamb, rotate it 90 degrees, and place it back on the grill on the same side. Cook for an additional 2 to 3 minutes, more marks appear. Flip the meat and move it to the medium side of the grill. Rotate the meat 90 degrees every 3 to 4 minutes, until a thermometer inserted into the center reads between 125° and 130°F.

Transfer the lamb to a wire rack to rest for at least 5 minutes.

While the lamb is resting, place the lettuce, radishes, and parmesan in large bowl. Add 3 to 4 tablespoons of the dressing and toss well. Season with pepper and scatter the chives and/or breadcrumbs on top, if you like. Serve with the sliced lamb.

Approximate total cook time for:

Lamb rib chops:
6 to 8 minutes

Lamb loin chops:
8 to 10 minutes

Boneless lamb leg pieces: 12 to 15 minutes, depending on size

SEA

Fish

Like beef, pork, and lamb, all types of fish are more alike than they are different. The particular species of fish that you cook in a given recipe really doesn't matter. The best fish that you can buy for any given recipe is the freshest one. So let that be your guide and your inspiration as you cook, rather than trying to track down a specific fish and compromising on quality, simply because the recipe said so.

You can think of fish in two main categories: mild flavored or full flavored. The distinction between those two groups has mostly to do with fat content. The higher in fat (when it comes to fish, we are generally talking about high-quality fats like omega-3s) a fish is, the stronger its flavor will be. Fattier fish are also known as "high-activity" fish, meaning they swim faster and travel greater distances throughout their lifetime. To employ a music analogy, the flavors of lean and fatty fish are made up of the same notes—fatty fish just play those notes at a higher volume.

No matter the type of fish you are cooking, you want to take care in the cooking process. When fish is fully cooked, it becomes flaky and will tend to fall apart on the grill or in the pan. That is why it's important to account for carryover cooking. Carryover cooking means that a food will continue to cook even after it has been removed from the heat source. Generally carryover cooking will cause the internal temperature of a protein to rise about 5°F after it comes off the heat. You want to remove fish before it is fully cooked so that carryover cooking can do the job of bringing the delicate fish to its perfect doneness.

Whether you're grilling, searing, or broiling, fish should be cooked with high heat. There are, of course, exceptions— poaching, for example—but most of the time cooking over high, direct heat is ideal because it helps to create a textured and flavorful exterior while leaving the interior tender and moist.

Properly cooking fish is not quite as simple as just throwing a fillet on a hot grill or sauté pan. But the following tips will help ensure success.

Mild-Flavored Fish

Cod

Grouper

Snapper

Flounder

Sea bass

Catfish

Tilapia

Mahi

Walleye

Sole

Fluke

Full-Flavored Fish

Salmon

Tuna

Mackerel

Swordfish

Cod

Halibut

Monkfish

Char

• When preparing to sear a piece of fish, the first decision regards the skin—will you leave it on or remove it? Fish skin, if not cooked properly, can turn into an unappetizing, slimy mess. But when properly cooked, the skin can be crisp and flavorful. Whether the skin is on or off also determines which side of the fillet will be cooked first: If you leave the skin on, then you must cook the skin side first. Deciding to cook fish skin on or off is a matter of preference. Properly cooking the skin takes a bit of practice, but is delicious when done right.

• Whether you sear, broil, or grill the fish, it is essential to begin with a very hot and well-oiled pan or grill or a preheated broiler. Fish cookery most often goes wrong because the fish sticks to the pan or the grill. This usually happens because moisture on the surface of the flesh cools the oil or cooking surface and causes sticking. Making sure that the fish is dry and that the cooking surface is properly oiled and as hot as possible will help prevent sticking.

• Dusting the fish with flour can help dry the skin and make it crisp, but too much flour will result in black, burned pieces, so be sure to pat off any excess flour before cooking. Also, do not salt the fish more than a couple minutes in advance, because the salt will draw moisture to the surface of the fillet. If this happens, be sure to pat fillets dry before cooking.

How to Grill, Broil, or Pan-Sear Fish

Season both sides of the fish with salt and pepper. Heat a grill to hot and oil the grates, preheat the broiler, or heat about 2 tablespoons oil in a sauté pan over medium-high to high heat. If you are cooking fish with the skin on, place the fillet with the skin toward the heat source: skin side down on a grill or in a sauté pan, skin side up for broiling. When searing fish in a pan, lay the fish in the hot oil carefully, letting it fall away from you so oil does not splash toward you. Immediately press the fish with the back of a flexible spatula to ensure that it is in full contact with the pan and the fillet remains flat. Hold the fish flat with firm pressure for 10 seconds. If you left the skin on, you will feel the skin tightening and trying to curl as soon as it hits the pan; use just enough pressure on the spatula to force the skin flat, but not so much that you crush the fish. If searing skinless fish, you will need only a light press with the spatula to ensure even contact with the pan.

Cook over high heat or broil for 3 to 4 minutes. When the edges of the fish begin to brown, flip the fish and cook for about 2 minutes more (depending on thickness and desired doneness).

The fish should be slightly translucent in the center when you remove it from the pan, broiler, or grill. Remember, it will continue to cook after it is removed from the heat. Allow the fish to rest for 2 minutes before serving.

PAN-SEARED FISH WITH BROCCOLI

breadcrumbs, broccoli, balsamic vinegar

This recipe is all about creating roasted aromas in different forms. Roasting broccoli in large pieces allows you to get browning and texture on the outside while keeping it tender with fresh aromas in the interior. Toasted breadcrumbs and balsamic vinegar add depth and texture that make this taste like a special-occasion meal even though it's easy enough for a busy weeknight supper.

SERVES 4

COMPOUND
(E,E)-2,4-heptadienal

AROMAS
fat fish, nut, plastic

Kosher salt SALT

1 head broccoli, quartered through the stem BITTER

1 tablespoon extra-virgin olive oil, plus more for brushing the broccoli FAT

Four 5-ounce mild white fish fillets UMAMI

2 tablespoons unsalted butter FAT

2 cloves garlic, peeled and smashed UMAMI

2 cups breadcrumbs

Grated lemon zest, for garnish SOUR

Fresh basil leaves, chopped if large, for garnish

2 tablespoons good-quality balsamic vinegar SOUR, SWEET

Preheat the broiler.

Bring a large pot of salted water to a rolling boil. Add the broccoli and cook for about 2 minutes, until partially tender. A knife inserted through the stem should have slight resistance. Remove from the water with a slotted spoon and set on a plate to drain and steam-dry.

Arrange the pieces of broccoli on a baking sheet with the cut sides facing up. Brush or spray the exposed face of the broccoli with olive oil and season with salt. Place under the broiler and cook until lightly charred, about 8 minutes.

Pan-sear the fish according to instructions on page 152. When the fish is finished cooking, remove it from the pan, drain any excess oil from the pan, and add the butter, olive oil, and garlic. Sauté until the garlic is golden on the edges, less than 30 seconds. Add the breadcrumbs and sauté until golden brown and crisped, 1 to 2 minutes. Remove the garlic breadcrumbs from the pan with a slotted spoon and set on paper towels to drain.

To serve, place one piece of fish on a plate with a broccoli piece next to it. Grate a few scrapes of lemon zest directly over the fish and broccoli, scatter a few basil leaves on top, drizzle each plate with ½ tablespoon balsamic vinegar, and garnish with breadcrumbs.

Fresh breadcrumbs are ideal for this recipe. These can be made by cutting day-old bread into cubes and pulsing them in a food processor, or by freezing the bread and grating it on a box grater.

FISH WITH BACON AND CREAMY TOMATO FARRO

tomato, farro, bacon, cream

Fish goes wonderfully with big toasted aromas. Farro contributes nuttiness, while bacon, tomato, and cream enhance the flavors of the grains and fish. Have fun with this recipe and try it out in different forms—for example, you can omit the bacon and substitute sautéed mushrooms. The farro without the fish makes a fantastic side to just about any protein or can be a satisfying meal all on its own.

SERVES 4

COMPOUND
2-heptanone

AROMAS
bell pepper, blue cheese, green, nut, spice

One 15-ounce can diced tomatoes, with their juice UMAMI

2 cups chicken stock

¼ pound thick-cut bacon, diced FAT, SALT, UMAMI

2 cloves garlic, peeled and smashed UMAMI

2 cups farro, rinsed and drained BITTER

2 teaspoons kosher salt SALT

½ cup heavy cream FAT

Freshly ground black pepper SPICY

Four 5-ounce mild or full flavored fish fillets UMAMI

1 teaspoon red wine vinegar SOUR

1 tablespoon chopped fresh basil, plus extra leaves for garnish

Halved cherry tomatoes, for garnish (optional) SWEET, UMAMI

Combine the diced tomatoes and chicken stock in a medium saucepot and bring to a boil. Once the mixture reaches a boil, turn the heat off but leave the pot on the stove.

Place a large sauté pan over medium heat, and put the bacon in it with 1 tablespoon water. Cook until the water evaporates and the bacon is browned and crisp.

Add the garlic and farro to the pan. Sauté for 1 minute, then stir in the tomato mixture and salt. Cover the pan and reduce the heat to medium-low. Simmer for 20 minutes or until all of the liquid has been absorbed.

Stir in the cream. Simmer 1 minute more, until thickened and creamy. Season to taste with salt and pepper. Re-cover to keep warm while you cook the fish.

Cook the fish following the instructions on page 152.

Just before serving, reheat the farro mixture if necessary and stir in the vinegar and basil. Spoon the farro into bowls and place the fish on top. Garnish with cherry tomatoes, if using, and basil leaves.

Adding water to the pan will actually make the bacon crisper: The water steams the bacon pieces, allowing them to begin cooking and rendering fat before they begin to brown, meaning more fat can be rendered from the bacon without burning the bacon.

FISH WITH LEMON-DILL LETTUCE SAUTÉ

fish, lettuce, lemon, dill

Sautéed lettuce may sound like a crazy idea, but it is a delicious and unexpected side that also just happens to be an ideal pairing for fish. Green aromas are a strong pairing for fish, and sautéing lettuce really brings those green aromas forward.

SERVES 4

COMPOUND
2,6-nonadienal

AROMAS
cucumber, green

---

1 pound new potatoes or fingerling potatoes UMAMI

Kosher salt SALT

Four 5-ounce mild white fish fillets UMAMI

2 tablespoons olive oil, plus more for garnish FAT

3 cloves garlic, peeled and smashed UMAMI

Pinch of red pepper flakes SPICY

1 teaspoon poppy seeds (optional) BITTER

1 head romaine lettuce, chopped

1 lemon, halved SOUR

1 tablespoon chopped fresh dill

Cut the potatoes in half or quarters, depending on their size (you want bite-size pieces). Place the potatoes in a large saucepot and add enough water to cover them by 1 to 2 inches. Season the water with a generous amount of salt. Place the pot over high heat and bring to a boil. When the water comes to a boil, cook for 2 to 4 minutes, until the potatoes are tender, then drain and spread the potatoes into a single layer on a baking sheet to steam-dry.

Cook the fish following the instructions on page 152.

In a large sauté pan, heat the oil, garlic, red pepper flakes, and poppy seeds (if using) over medium-high heat. When the garlic begins to sizzle and lightly brown at the edges, add the potatoes and stir well. Allow the potatoes to settle in the pan and brown on one side.

Add the romaine and cook for about 1 minute more, until the lettuce is partially wilted. Remove the pan from the heat and squeeze in fresh lemon juice to taste. Season with salt and stir in the dill.

Serve the lettuce and potatoes with the fish and drizzle each plate with olive oil.

The potatoes will likely not be cooked through completely at this stage. That's okay; they will cook more in the next step. If they are on the larger side, they may need to boil for up to 4 minutes. If they start to turn white at the edges, remove them immediately, as that is a sign the potatoes are beginning to overcook.

MILK-POACHED FISH WITH BASIL

fish, milk, onion, basil

"Fat equals flavor" is an age-old saying; and it's true, but not quite in the way that you think. You see, fat brings flavor, but it's more of a transport vehicle than a creator. Fat is the ultimate way to capture aromas and deliver them from one food to another. In this recipe, milk takes all the lovely aromas from butter, lemon, herbs, and alliums and deposits them in your fish fillets.

SERVES 4

COMPOUND
2-heptanone

AROMAS
bell pepper, blue cheese, fruit, green, nut, spice

Four 5-ounce meaty white fish fillets (such as grouper, halibut, tilefish, cod, or sea bass), skin removed UMAMI

Kosher salt SALT

4 tablespoons (½ stick) unsalted butter FAT

1 tablespoon olive oil FAT

2 shallots, thinly sliced

4 cloves garlic, thinly sliced UMAMI

2 teaspoons all-purpose flour, or a gluten-free alternative

2 cups whole or 2% milk, plus more as needed FAT

Zest of 1 lemon, removed in strips with a vegetable peeler

4 branches fresh basil, plus whole leaves for garnish

½ teaspoon freshly ground black pepper, plus more as needed SPICY

Season the fish fillets with salt. Set aside on a plate.

Melt the butter in a large sauté pan over medium-high heat. Cook until the butter is lightly browned and has a roasted, nutty aroma, about 4 minutes.

Add the oil to the butter. Pat the fish fillets dry and place them in the pan, skin side facing up. Cook until well browned on the bottom, about 3 minutes. Remove the fillets from the pan and place them back on the plate.

Add the shallots and garlic to the pan and sauté for 2 to 3 minutes, until lightly browned. Add the flour and stir until blended. Cook, stirring constantly, for 1 minute. Gradually whisk in the milk and bring to a simmer. Add the lemon zest, basil, 2 teaspoons salt, the pepper, and nutmeg.

Return the fish to the pan and bring the milk back to a simmer, then reduce the heat slightly. (For proper poaching you're looking to maintain the temperature between 160° and 180°F.) Poach the fillets for 12 to 15 minutes, until they are just cooked through.

No need to pull out a thermometer here: If the milk is completely still and barely steaming, the temperature is a bit too low; if it is bubbling consistently all over the pan, the heat is a bit too high. Partially covering the pan can help keep the temperature more consistent.

2 scrapes freshly grated nutmeg

1 tablespoon capers, drained

SALT

Fresh lemon juice

Chopped toasted almonds or toasted breadcrumbs, for garnish (optional)

Remove the fish from the pan and place a portion on each plate. Taste the poaching liquid for seasoning and consistency and add salt and pepper to taste. If the sauce seems too thin (it should coat the back of a spoon), simmer to reduce it. Remove the basil branches and take the pan off of the heat. Stir in the capers, lemon juice to taste, and more basil. Garnish with nuts or bread-crumbs, if you like.

PAN-SEARED FISH WITH BROWN BUTTER AND GRAPE VINAIGRETTE

brown butter, fennel, grapes

Grapes and brown butter are not your standard accompaniment to fish, but digging into the unexpected can yield delicious combinations—their flavors are an incredible match. Browning the butter in a separate pan gives it a deep, rich roasted flavor that is the perfect bridge between the fish and the grapes.

SERVES 4

COMPOUND
2,3-butanediol

AROMAS
fruit, herb, onion

---

1 tablespoon kosher salt SALT

1 teaspoon fennel seeds

½ teaspoon freshly ground black pepper SPICY

1 tablespoon vegetable oil FAT

Four 5-ounce fish steaks or fillets (such as tuna, swordfish, or salmon) UMAMI

8 tablespoons (1 stick) unsalted butter FAT

1 shallot, thinly sliced, or 2 tablespoons sliced scallion, white and light green parts only

3 or 4 branches fresh thyme

1 cup halved seedless grapes SWEET

¼ cup white wine vinegar SOUR

In a small bowl, mix together the salt, fennel seeds, and pepper. Season the fish well on both sides with the spice mixture.

Heat the oil in a large sauté pan over high heat. Carefully add the fish to the pan and reduce the heat to medium-high. When well browned on one side, flip and brown on the second side.

While the fish is cooking, melt the butter in a small saucepot over medium heat. The butter will melt, then boil. Continue cooking until the butter takes on a light amber color, 3 to 4 minutes, then remove from the heat and set aside.

When the fish is finished cooking, transfer to a wire rack to rest. Drain the oil from the pan, leaving behind about 1 teaspoon oil. Add the shallots and sauté until tender, about 2 minutes. Add the thyme and grapes and continue cooking until the grapes begin to soften, 2 to 3 minutes more. Pour in the vinegar and remove the pan from the heat. Stir in the butter and mix well.

Remove and discard the thyme. Serve the fish with the grapes and butter sauce spooned over the top.

Cook tuna 1 to 2 minutes per side for rare to medium-rare; cook salmon for 3 to 4 minutes per side for medium; swordfish should be cooked medium-well, 4 to 5 minutes per side.

Remember that butter will turn 1 or 2 shades darker after it is removed from the heat.

MISO AND MAPLE–GLAZED FISH

maple syrup, miso, vinegar

This is an amped-up version of a recipe that built an empire, inspired by the miso-glazed fish at the iconic restaurant Nobu. Big, bold flavors and layered Maillard aromas that come from miso, maple syrup, and smoked paprika make this a real crowd-pleaser. The glaze mixture can be made in bigger batches and stored for up to 10 days in the refrigerator, so this recipe could easily wind up in heavy rotation at your house. Serve with Coco-Slaw (page 19) or A Different Kind of Green Salad (page 28).

SERVES 4

COMPOUND
phenol

AROMAS
medicinal, phenol, sharp, smoke, spice

2 tablespoons white miso SALT, UMAMI

1 tablespoon plus 1 teaspoon rice vinegar SOUR

1 tablespoon maple syrup SWEET

Finely grated zest of 1 lime

1 teaspoon smoked paprika

Pinch of cayenne pepper SPICY

Four 5-ounce fish fillets (such as salmon, cod, black cod, or halibut) UMAMI

Combine the miso, rice vinegar, maple syrup, lime zest, paprika, and cayenne in a large zip-top plastic bag. Mix thoroughly. Add the fish to the bag, squeeze out all the air, seal the bag, and gently turn to coat completely. Refrigerate the fish to marinate for at least 2 hours or up to overnight.

Preheat the broiler. Set a wire rack over a baking sheet and spray the rack with nonstick cooking spray.

Remove the fish from the bag and wipe off any excess marinade. Arrange the fish on the rack and place in the oven beneath the broiler on a rack positioned in the center of the oven.

Broil until the fish is well browned on top and cooked through, about 12 minutes. Remove from the oven and rest for 1 minute on the pan before serving.

FISH WITH SWEET PEA AND HAM QUINOA PILAF

peas, mushrooms, ham

This recipe is based on the strong pairing between fish and toasted nuts. Rather than adding nuts to the dish, we let quinoa stand in.

SERVES 4

COMPOUND
acetophenone

AROMAS
almond, flower, meat, must, plastic

¼ pound sliced smoked ham or bacon FAT, SALT, UMAMI

3 tablespoons unsalted butter FAT

8 ounces cremini mushrooms, cleaned and finely chopped UMAMI

1 tablespoon chopped garlic UMAMI

1 cup quinoa, rinsed and drained BITTER

One 16-pound package frozen green peas, thawed

2 cups chicken stock or water

1 tablespoon chopped fresh mint

2 tablespoons olive oil FAT

2 teaspoons white wine vinegar or lemon juice ACID

Kosher salt SALT

Freshly ground black pepper SPICY

Four 5-ounce mild white fish fillets UMAMI

Stack the ham slices on a cutting board and cut them in half, then cut crosswise into thin strips so that each piece is no more than 3 inches long and ¼ inch wide.

Melt the butter in a large sauté pan over high heat. When the butter begins to foam, add the ham and sauté briefly until lightly browned at the edges, 1 to 2 minutes.

Add the mushrooms and garlic. Sauté, stirring often, until no liquid remains in the pan and the mushrooms are lightly browned, 4 to 5 minutes.

Reduce the heat to medium and add the quinoa. Stir well and continue cooking until the grains begin to sizzle or pop, about 1 minute. Add the peas and chicken stock and bring to a simmer. Cook until all the liquid has been absorbed, about 12 minutes. Remove from the heat and stir in the mint, olive oil, and vinegar. Season to taste with salt and pepper.

Meanwhile, cook the fish according to the instructions on page 152.

To serve, spoon the pilaf onto plates and top with the fish.

At this point it may seem like you've got way too much butter in the pan, but don't worry, you haven't.

FENNEL-SEARED FISH WITH GREEN BEANS, SESAME, AND DILL

fennel, green beans, sesame, dill

SERVES 4

COMPOUND
(Z)-3-hexen-1-ol

AROMAS
bell pepper, grass, green, herb, unripe banana

Dill and fennel work very well together. But this dish is all about getting those aromas to work together in different forms—the toasted aromas from the fennel seeds and the freshness from the dill are then layered with more fresh and green aromas from the green beans and more toasted ones from the sesame seeds.

Kosher salt SALT

½ cup mayonnaise FAT

2 tablespoons soy sauce SALT, UMAMI

2 teaspoons tomato paste UMAMI

1 teaspoon sesame oil (optional) FAT, UMAMI

1 teaspoon sriracha, or more to taste SPICY

1 pound green beans, trimmed

Four 5-ounce portions firm white fish (such as salmon, tuna, halibut, grouper, or bass)

½ teaspoon ground fennel seeds

4 tablespoons olive oil FAT

1 fennel bulb, sliced

1 tablespoon chopped fresh dill

2 tablespoons toasted sesame seeds

Bring a large pot of salted water to a boil. Make an ice bath in a large bowl with water and ice.

In a small bowl, whisk together the mayonnaise, 1 tablespoon of the soy sauce, the tomato paste, sesame oil (if using), and sriracha. Season to taste with salt and more sriracha, if you like.

Add the green beans to the boiling water and cook until just tender, about 2½ minutes. Remove the green beans with a slotted spoon and plunge them into the ice water to chill quickly. When cooled, drain, transfer to a large clean bowl, and set aside.

Season the fish with salt on both sides and season the fish on the non-skin side only with the fennel seed. Set aside.

Heat 2 tablespoons of the olive oil in a large sauté pan over medium-high heat. When the pan is hot and the oil begins to shimmer, pat the fish dry, then add it to the pan, fennel-seasoned side up. Gently shake the pan, then leave the fish to sear undisturbed for 2 minutes.

Reduce the heat to medium and scatter the sliced fennel over the fish. Cook until well browned, up to 2 minutes more, then flip the fish. Cook for 1 minute, then check for doneness. Continue

continued

Juice of 1 lemon SOUR

Cherry tomatoes, for garnish

Jarred crispy shallots, for garnish (optional)

cooking until the fish is cooked through. Transfer the fish to plates and keep warm until you're ready to serve.

Add the remaining 1 tablespoon of soy sauce, the dill, and sesame seeds to the green beans. Toss well to combine. Add the remaining 2 tablespoons olive oil and the lemon juice. Mix again and adjust the seasoning if needed.

To serve, spread a spoonful of the mayonnaise sauce on each plate. Top with the fish, and arrange the green beans next to the fish. Garnish with tomatoes and crispy shallots, if using.

FISH WITH SWEET POTATO–POBLANO HASH

sweet potato, mushrooms, basil, honey, mustard

This is probably the boldest fish recipe you will find in this book. It is somehow comfort food but light and fresh at the same time. Jamie says this dish reminds him of Brooke—a little bit spicy and a little bit sweet. We think you'll fall in love with the sweet potato hash, which is an incredible side dish for just about anything.

SERVES 4

COMPOUND
2-ethyl-1-hexanol

AROMAS
citrus, green, oil, rose

2 large sweet potatoes, cut into 1-inch cubes (4 to 5 cups) SWEET

8 ounces cremini mushrooms, cleaned and quartered UMAMI

4 cloves garlic, peeled and smashed UMAMI

4 branches fresh thyme

1 teaspoon kosher salt SALT

3 tablespoons olive oil, plus more for garnish FAT

Four 5-ounce portions firm white fish (such as halibut, grouper, or bass)

1 poblano chile, diced SPICY

1 tablespoon minced garlic UMAMI

2 tablespoons apple cider vinegar SOUR

1 tablespoon honey SWEET

2 teaspoons Dijon mustard SPICY

1 tablespoon chopped fresh basil, plus small leaves for garnish

¼ cup toasted pumpkin or sunflower seeds (optional)

Preheat the oven to 400°F.

Combine the sweet potatoes, mushrooms, smashed garlic, thyme, salt, and 2 tablespoons of the olive oil in a bowl. Toss well to mix, then spread in a single layer on a baking sheet. Place on the center rack of the oven and roast until tender and lightly browned, about 12 minutes.

Pan-sear the fish following the instructions on page 152. Set the fish aside on a plate, covered with aluminum foil to keep warm. Discard the fat from the pan and wipe clean.

In the same sauté pan, heat the remaining 1 tablespoon olive oil over medium heat. Add the poblano and minced garlic and cook, stirring often, until the chile is tender, 4 to 6 minutes.

While the chile cooks, mix together the vinegar, honey, mustard, and basil.

Add the roasted sweet potatoes and mushrooms to the sauté pan and toss well to coat. Adjust the seasoning with salt and pepper. Remove the pan from the heat and add the honey-mustard mixture to the pan. Mix well.

Serve the sweet potatoes with the fish, garnished with a drizzle of olive oil, some basil leaves, and the pumpkin seeds, if using.

FISH WITH SPICED POTATOES AND AVOCADO CREAM

potato, tomato, avocado

This recipe is all about the all-too-interesting-to-ignore pairing of avocado and potatoes. First you roast potatoes and cherry tomatoes together in one pan. Then you make a thick, creamy dressing from avocado to serve alongside the potatoes and fish. Plated, it's an elegant presentation . . . or wrap that whole thing up in a tortilla for some killer fish tacos!

SERVES 4

COMPOUND
diacetyl

AROMAS
butter, caramel, fruit, pastry

1 pound new potatoes or fingerling potatoes UMAMI

2 teaspoons cumin seeds

2 teaspoons garlic powder

1 teaspoon ground turmeric BITTER

¼ cup extra-virgin olive oil FAT

1 cup halved cherry tomatoes UMAMI, SWEET

Kosher salt SALT

¼ red onion, sliced as thin as possible

¼ cup red wine vinegar SOUR

½ teaspoon sugar SWEET

1 avocado, pitted, peeled, and cut into cubes FAT

½ cup sour cream FAT, SOUR

1 tablespoon minced fresh cilantro, plus more leaves for garnish (optional)

1 teaspoon sriracha or other hot sauce SPICY

Preheat the oven to 425°F.

Cut the potatoes in half or quarters, depending on their size (you want bite-size pieces). Place the potatoes in a bowl and add the cumin seeds, garlic powder, turmeric, and olive oil.

Toss well to coat. Spread the potatoes out in a single layer on a baking sheet. They should not touch one another; if there is not enough room, divide between two pans. Make sure the potatoes are arranged so that the flat, cut side of the potato is facing down on the pan. Sprinkle 2 teaspoons salt evenly over the potatoes and immediately place them in the oven.

Let the potatoes roast undisturbed for 8 minutes. Add the tomatoes to the pan and return to the oven to roast for about 8 minutes more, until the potatoes are tender. Use a spatula to stir the vegetables, then set aside to cool slightly.

While the potatoes and tomatoes roast, combine the vinegar, sugar, and a pinch of salt in a small bowl; stir until the salt is dissolved. Add the onion, mix well, and set aside until you're ready to serve.

Salt draws water out of food. Adding the salt at the last moment will help ensure that the potatoes get crisp and brown in the oven; adding it too soon could make the surface of the potatoes moist and cause them to steam, rather than roast.

½ teaspoon ground cumin

Juice of 1 lime SOUR

**Four 5-ounce portions fish
(mild or full flavored)**

1 cup baby arugula leaves
BITTER, SPICY

**Sliced radishes, for garnish
(optional)** SPICY

Combine the avocado, sour cream, minced cilantro (if using), hot sauce, ground cumin, and lime juice in a bowl and mash with a fork or whisk until smooth, or blend in a food processor.

Pan-sear, broil, or grill the fish following the instructions on page 152.

Drain the vinegar from the onions, leaving the onions in the bowl. Add the roasted potatoes and tomatoes to the bowl large bowl. And toss well to combine.

Serve the potato mixture with the fish, a large dollop of the avocado dressing, and the arugula. Garnish with cilantro leaves and radishes, if desired.

Shrimp, Crab, and Lobster

There is one simple rule for cooking crustaceans: less is more. All crustaceans—shrimp, lobster, crab, crawfish, langoustine—have little fat or connective tissue, meaning they can go from perfect to tough and rubbery in a matter of moments. The quicker they can be cooked, the better they will be. This also means that if being served hot, they should not be cooked until moments before being served. Keeping any crustaceans hot for an extended period of time will cause them to become dry and tough.

When boiling crustaceans, it is best to cook them with their shells on, then peel and devein after cooking. It's not the easiest option, but when cooking shrimp without their shells, the water can dry out the meat of the shrimp, leaving them with a mealy texture. When using dry-heat cooking methods like sautéing or grilling, it is fine to cook them with the shells already removed. Though with all dry-heat methods, make sure they are well coated with fat (oil or butter) to protect the flesh from the direct heat, which can toughen the exterior.

The flavor of crustaceans comes mainly from nitrogen-containing compounds known as amines and thiazines. Amines are derived from ammonia and thiazines also contain a sulphur atom. These compounds are responsible for the "fishy" and ammonia-like odors associated with seafood that is past its prime. Fresh fish and shellfish should have little or no smell, or should smell like the ocean. But if they have been stored in a closed plastic container, their odor can become more pronounced even if they have not gone bad. To check, pat the items dry and give them another sniff in a clean air space. If the strong smell remains, it is probably best not to eat them.

CHILLED CARROT SOUP WITH POACHED SHRIMP

carrot, ginger, red wine

Carrots, ginger, and lime are an outstanding combination all on their own. In this recipe, they make an awesome soup that is delicious served hot or cold. The additional of fresh poached shrimp takes this combo to the next level both in flavor and presentation. The sharp, "pine-y" aromas in carrots, lime, and ginger are all a great match for shrimp flavor-wise. The soup and the shrimp can both be prepared a day or two in advance.

SERVES 4

COMPOUND
terpinolene

AROMAS
pine, plastic, sweet

2 tablespoons extra-virgin olive oil, plus 2 to 3 tablespoons for garnish FAT

2 teaspoons fresh lime juice, plus juice of 2 limes SOUR

1 teaspoon chopped fresh cilantro

Pinch of kosher salt SALT

Freshly ground black pepper SPICY

About 1 pound fresh shrimp, shell on UMAMI

2 cups chicken stock

2 tablespoons olive oil FAT

4 cloves garlic, chopped UMAMI

1 teaspoon ground coriander

1 cup minced onion (about ½ medium onion)

In a medium bowl, combine the extra-virgin olive oil, 2 teaspoons lime juice, cilantro, salt, and pepper. Mix well and set aside.

Rinse the shrimp, with their shells on, under cold water. Bring the chicken stock to a boil in a medium saucepot, add the shrimp, and stir once. Put a tight-fitting lid on the pot, then turn the heat off and let the pot stand for 5 minutes.

Remove the shrimp from the pot with a slotted spoon and place on a large plate or baking sheet to cool (do not submerge them in water). Set aside the chicken stock.

When the shrimp are cool enough to handle, peel and devein them. Add them to the lime dressing and toss to coat. Set aside until you're ready to serve, or cover and refrigerate if not serving the same day.

Heat the olive oil, garlic, and coriander in a wide saucepot over medium-high heat. When the spices begin to sizzle and become aromatic, add the onion and sauté until translucent, about 6 minutes, stirring often. Reduce the heat as needed to prevent the onion from browning.

continued

2-inch piece fresh ginger, peeled and thinly sliced SPICY

4 cups thinly sliced carrots (about 6 medium carrots) SWEET

2 teaspoons kosher salt SALT

1 cup heavy cream FAT

1 avocado FAT

Add the ginger, carrots, and kosher salt and stir well. Cook, stirring often, until the carrots are slightly softened, about 5 minutes. If the vegetables begin to brown, reduce the heat or add water a tablespoon at a time to prevent browning. Add the reserved stock and simmer until the liquid is reduced by half, about 6 minutes more.

When the carrots are very tender, transfer the mixture to a blender and purée until smooth. Return the purée to the pot and stir in the cream. Bring the soup to a boil and stir in the juice of 2 limes, or to taste. Adjust the seasoning with salt and pepper. Transfer to a large bowl set over another bowl filled with ice water and stir until completely chilled. Alternatively, chill the soup in the refrigerator for a few hours or up to 2 days.

Just before serving, pit, peel, and slice the avocado. Serve the soup garnished with the shrimp, avocado, and a drizzle of good-quality olive oil.

The carrots are going to be puréed so they need to be completely soft. To check doneness, remove one piece of carrot with a spoon and try to smash it on a cutting board with the back of the spoon. If it does not crush easily, continue cooking until it does.

CREAMY SHRIMP PASTA WITH CHARRED TOMATO AND PUMPKIN

shrimp, pumpkin, cream, bread, pasta

Shrimp and pumpkin are one of the more intriguing flavor pairings we've found. They both have a subtle sweetness and rich, buttery aromas, making them a great match in both taste and flavor. We just can't resist it in the form of this delicious fall pasta, which is hearty, yet light.

SERVES 4

COMPOUND
2,3-pentanedione

AROMAS
bitter, butter, caramel, cream, fruit, sweet

1 beefsteak tomato UMAMI

2 cloves garlic, peeled UMAMI

4 to 6 fresh basil leaves

2 cups chicken stock

3 tablespoons unsalted butter FAT

1 cup finely chopped yellow onion (about ½ medium onion)

2 cups diced peeled, seeded pumpkin or butternut squash SWEET

1 teaspoon dried sage

½ cup dry white wine ACID

8 ounces dried mezze rigatoni or rigatoni

2 teaspoons kosher salt SALT

1 pound fresh shrimp, peeled and deveined UMAMI

½ cup heavy cream FAT

½ cup toasted breadcrumbs

Cut the tomato in half and char the cut side underneath a preheated broiler or in a lightly oiled cast-iron skillet over medium-high heat.

Transfer the tomato to a medium saucepot and add the garlic, basil, and chicken stock. Bring to a boil, then cover, remove from the heat, and set aside for 15 minutes to infuse.

Strain the stock through a fine-mesh strainer into a bowl. Press the tomatoes with the back of spoon to crush them and extract as much liquid as possible. Set aside the liquid and discard the basil, garlic, and remaining tomato solids.

While the stock is infusing, start the pasta. Melt 2 tablespoons of the butter in a wide-bottomed saucepot over medium-high heat. Add the onion and sauté until translucent and tender, without browning, about 6 minutes.

For breadcrumbs that are perfectly crispy and chewy, melt 2 tablespoons butter in a sauté pan over medium heat. Add the breadcrumbs and pinch of kosher salt and cook, stirring constantly, until they are golden brown. Drain on paper towels. To really kick things up, add a smashed garlic clove to the butter while it is melting and leave it in the pan while the breadcrumbs toast.

Adding a pinch of salt to the onion as it cooks will draw out a little water and help it soften without browning.

When the onions are translucent, add the remaining 1 tablespoon butter, the pumpkin, and sage. Sauté for about 2 minutes, until the pumpkin is slightly softened. Deglaze the pan with the white wine and cook until nearly dry.

Stir in the dried pasta and mix well. Add the reserved chicken stock, 2 cups water, and the salt. Bring to a simmer, then cover the pot. Cook, stirring occasionally, until the pasta is nearly tender, about 8 minutes.

Remove the lid from the pot and turn the heat to high. Add the shrimp and cream, and cook, stirring constantly, until the shrimp are cooked though, 3 to 4 minutes.

Serve garnished with the breadcrumbs.

At this point the sauce should be thick and creamy; if it is not, remove the shrimp to keep them from overcooking and continue boiling until the sauce thickens.

BRAZILIAN SHRIMP AND COCONUT STEW

shrimp, tomato, coconut, pepper

Tomato + coconut + shrimp is a stunningly delicious combination. Together they can make a simple meal feel like an escape to the tropics. This recipe is made in the style of *moqueca,* the famed seafood stew of Bahia, Brazil, which we learned to cook when we spent two weeks as the chefs-in-residence at the idyllic UXUA Hotel and Casas in Trancoso.

SERVES 4

COMPOUND
hexanal

AROMAS
fresh, fruit, grass, green, oil

1¹/₂ pounds fresh shrimp, peeled and deveined UMAMI

Kosher salt SALT

2 tablespoons vegetable oil FAT

1 teaspoon paprika

2 cloves garlic, peeled and smashed UMAMI

¹/₂ cup diced red bell pepper SWEET

¹/₂ cup diced onion

¹/₂ jalapeño chile, diced SPICY

¹/₂ cup diced tomato UMAMI

One 13.5- or 14-ounce can coconut milk FAT

1 tablespoon chopped fresh flat-leaf parsley

1 tablespoon chopped fresh cilantro

Fresh lemon juice SOUR

Freshly ground black pepper SPICY

2 cups cooked rice, or toasted or grilled bread for serving (optional)

¹/₄ cup toasted quinoa or croutons, for garnish (optional)

Season the shrimp with 1¹/₂ teaspoons salt and set aside.

Combine the oil, paprika, and garlic in a large sauté pan over medium heat. When the garlic sizzles and begins to brown at the edges, pat the shrimp dry and add to the pan. Cook on one side for 30 seconds, then flip and cook for 30 seconds longer on the second side. Transfer the shrimp to a clean plate next to the stove.

Add the bell pepper, onion, and jalapeño to the hot pan and sauté for 2 to 3 minutes, until tender. Stir in the tomatoes and mix well. Add the coconut milk and bring to a simmer. Cook at a low simmer for 2 to 3 minutes, until slightly thickened.

Return the shrimp to the pan and add the parsley and cilantro. Simmer until the shrimp are just cooked through, about 4 minutes. Remove from the heat and season to taste with lemon juice, salt, and pepper.

If desired, serve over rice or bread and garnish with toasted quinoa or croutons.

The shrimp will not be fully cooked at this point; they will finish cooking later.

LUMP CRAB BRUSCHETTA

tomato, sesame, dill, toast

Pan con tomate is one of the essential foods of Spain: crisp slices of bread, still tender on the inside, saturated with garlic, tomato, and olive oil. We really didn't think it could get any better. Then it did. . . . Looking at some ways to have some fun with the strong pairing between crab and tomato, we decided to top pan con tomate with a creamy, herby crab salad. It is summer eating perfection.

SERVES 6 to 8

COMPOUND
2-ethyl-1-hexanol

AROMAS
citrus, green, oil, rose

Grated zest and juice of ½ lemon SOUR

2 teaspoons chopped fresh dill

¼ cup mayonnaise FAT

1 pound lump crabmeat, picked over for shells and cartilage UMAMI

Kosher salt SALT

Freshly ground black pepper SPICY

4 large slices country-style sourdough or semolina bread

2 tablespoons extra-virgin olive oil FAT

1 garlic clove, peeled UMAMI

1 large ripe beefsteak tomato, halved UMAMI

2 tablespoons toasted sesame seeds

Combine the lemon zest and juice, dill, and mayonnaise in a large bowl and mix well. Add the crabmeat and gently fold to combine. Season to taste with salt and pepper. Cover and refrigerate until you're ready to serve, up to 24 hours.

Heat a grill to medium-high and oil the grates, or preheat the broiler.

Brush the bread with a generous amount of olive oil on both sides. Toast on the grill or under the broiler until charred at the edges.

Transfer the bread to a wire rack and rub one side of each slice with the garlic clove. Then rub the same side with the cut side of the tomato, gently crushing the tomato in your hand as you scrape it across the bread.

Top the tomato-soaked bread with the dressed crab and sprinkle with the sesame seeds. Serve immediately.

Imagine the crisp bread is like a cheese grater and you are trying to grate the tomato. The goal is to break down the tomato and get it to soak into the bread.

CRAB AND CRISP APPLE SALAD

apple, mayonnaise, chive, lime

The tart crunch of the apple is essential in this dish. The crab can be dressed and seasoned up to a day in advance, but do not add the apples until immediately before serving. It can be served as an hors d'oeuvre or an appetizer. To serve as an hors d'oeuvre, finely dice the apple, mix it into the crab, and place a spoonful of the mixture on top of toasted crostini. To serve as an appetizer, gently mound ¼ cup of the crab mixture in the center of a plate and tuck 4 or 5 thin slices of apple into each mound of crab.

SERVES 6 to 8

COMPOUND
caprylaldehyde

AROMAS
citrus, fat, floral, green, pungent

Grated zest and juice of ½ lime
SOUR

2 teaspoons chopped fresh chives

¼ teaspoon celery seed BITTER

2 tablespoons mayonnaise FAT

1 pound lump crabmeat, picked over for shells and cartilage
UMAMI

Kosher salt SALT

Freshly ground black pepper
SPICY

1 Granny Smith apple SOUR, SWEET

Combine the lime zest and juice, chives, celery seed, and mayonnaise in a large bowl and mix well. Add the crabmeat and gently fold to combine. Season to taste with salt and pepper. Cover and refrigerate until you're ready to serve, up to 24 hours.

Shortly before serving, finely dice or thinly slice the apple. Fold the diced apple into the crab mixture, or serve the crab with the apple slices as described above.

GRILLED LOBSTER AND BUTTERNUT SQUASH WITH TOMATO, OLIVE, AND PRESERVED LEMON RELISH

lobster, butternut squash, olive, tomato

Deep roasted Maillard aromas are the common link between lobster, butternut squash, olives, and tomato. This recipe amplifies those flavors by seasoning both lobster and squash with smoked paprika and sage, then cooking them on the grill. The result is smoky, delicious, and completely unexpected.

SERVES 4

COMPOUND
2,5-dimethylpyrazine

AROMAS
burnt plastic, cocoa, medicinal, roast beef, toasted nut

1 tablespoon kosher salt SALT

1 teaspoon smoked paprika

1 teaspoon dried sage

4 lobster tails, shell on (1½ to 2 pounds), split lengthwise and deveined UMAMI

1 medium butternut squash (about 2½ pounds), peeled, seeded, and sliced into rounds ½ inch thick SWEET

¼ cup extra-virgin olive oil, plus more as needed FAT

½ cup halved cherry tomatoes SWEET, UMAMI

¼ cup pitted Castelvetrano or picholine olives, SALT, UMAMI

2 tablespoons red wine vinegar SOUR

2 teaspoons minced preserved lemon or grated zest of 1 lemon BITTER, SOUR, SWEET

1 cup baby arugula BITTER, SPICY

Toasted pine nuts, for garnish (optional)

Thinly sliced red onion, for garnish (optional)

Heat a grill to hot and oil the grates.

Combine the salt, paprika, and sage in a small bowl and mix well. Brush the lobster tails and butternut squash with olive oil and season with the salt mixture.

Place the lobster tails, cut side down, on the grill. Cook for 4 minutes, then flip and cook for 5 to 6 minutes more, until the meat is no longer translucent in the center. Remove from the grill and place on a wire rack to cool slightly.

Grill the butternut squash at the same time as the lobster tails, flipping every 2 minutes until easily pierced through the center with the tip of a knife, 6 to 8 minutes total.

Arrange the grilled lobster and squash together on a platter. Combine the tomatoes, olives, olive oil, vinegar, and lemon in a bowl and mix well. Spoon the mixture over the lobster and squash. Garnish with the baby arugula and, if desired, pine nuts and onion.

DRINKS

Crafting drinks had long been a hobby of ours, but after having two children it became a necessity. There is nothing that we enjoy more than sitting down with a simple cocktail at the end of the day. (We also share four nonalcoholic favorites starting on page 195.)

Drinks, more so than any other food item, rely on aromas to convey flavor. *The Flavor Matrix* showed how aromatic compounds (those things that create flavor) are part of a larger group called volatile compounds. Volatile compounds are just that—volatile—meaning that they readily dissipate into the air. Aromas from herbs, spices, and fresh produce can only be held onto for so long before they vanish. Yet still, most of our favorite sips rely a good deal on fresh fruits, vegetables, and herbs. These recipes are mere suggestions; feel encouraged to substitute fruits, vegetables, and herbs based on the season or whatever you may have on hand.

COCOA AND LEMON OLD FASHIONED

cocoa, whiskey, lemon

This drink brings in citrus aromas in two forms: The aromatic peel of the orange pairs perfectly with the citrus notes in cocoa. Then lemon adds brightness and acidity to the cocktail.

MAKES about 1 cup syrup, enough for about 45 drinks

COMPOUND
alpha-phellandrene

AROMAS
citrus, mint, black pepper, turpentine, wood

COCOA SYRUP

1/2 cup sugar SWEET

2 tablespoons unsweetened cocoa powder BITTER

Zest of 1 orange, removed in strips with a vegetable peeler BITTER, SWEET

FOR EACH COCKTAIL

1 teaspoon Cocoa Syrup BITTER, SWEET

1 1/2 ounces (3 tablespoons) whiskey

1 wedge lemon SOUR

1 ounce (2 tablespoons) club soda

Lemon twist, for garnish

Make the cocoa syrup: Combine the sugar and cocoa in a medium saucepot, whisking thoroughly. Whisk in 1 cup water. Bring to a boil and cook, stirring gently, until the sugar and cocoa have dissolved, 6 to 8 minutes.

Remove the pot from the heat. Add the orange zest to the hot syrup and set aside to cool to room temperature. When cooled, transfer to an airtight container and store in the refrigerator for up to 3 months.

To make 1 cocktail: Fill a rocks glass halfway with ice cubes. Add the cocoa syrup and whiskey. Squeeze in the juice from the lemon wedge (about 1 teaspoon, or to taste) and stir to thoroughly chill. Top with the club soda and garnish with a lemon twist.

Cocoa powder has a tendency to form clumps when added to liquid. Whisking it together with the sugar before adding the water will help prevent this.

SPICED BUTTERNUT SQUASH OLD FASHIONED

bourbon, butternut squash

We'd love to take credit for coming up with this incredible pairing, which we also featured in *The Flavor Matrix.* However, we first sampled a version of this cocktail at the bar of the restaurant Redd in Yountville, CA (which has since closed). In the years that have passed since first tasting it, Jamie has tinkered with the recipe until finally arriving at this spice-laden version, which remains a staple on our refrigerator shelf throughout the fall.

MAKES 2½ cups coulis, enough for 20 cocktails

COMPOUND 2-acetyalfuran

AROMAS balsamic, cocoa, coffee, smoke, tobacco

SPICED BUTTERNUT SQUASH COULIS

1 teaspoon coriander seeds

1 teaspoon whole cloves

1 teaspoon black peppercorns SPICY

2 cinnamon sticks

Grated zest of ½ lemon BITTER, SWEET

1 teaspoon kosher salt SALT

2 cups cubed peeled and seeded butternut squash SWEET

FOR EACH COCKTAIL

1 ounce (2 tablespoons) Spiced Butternut Squash Coulis SWEET

1½ ounces (3 tablespoons) bourbon SWEET

Club soda, for serving

Lemon twist, for garnish

Make the coulis: Tie the coriander, cloves, and peppercorns in a cheesecloth sachet, or put them in a tea ball or bag. Add them to 2 cups water in a medium saucepot, then add the cinnamon, lemon zest, and salt. Bring the mixture to a simmer. Add the butternut squash and cook until the squash is tender, about 10 minutes.

Pour the mixture into a strainer over a bowl to catch the cooking liquid. Discard the spices. Transfer the squash cubes to a blender and pour in ½ cup of the cooking liquid. Purée until smooth, adding more of the liquid as needed for a smooth consistency. Store the coulis in an airtight container in the refrigerator for up to 2 weeks.

To make 1 cocktail: Combine the coulis and bourbon in a shaker filled halfway with ice cubes. Shake to chill thoroughly. Strain into a rocks glass filled with ice cubes. Top with club soda and garnish with a lemon twist.

MEZCAL MICHELADA

mezcal, beer, coriander

Using freshly ground coriander really makes all the difference in this recipe, as it brings powerful citrus aromas that are seriously lacking in jars of ground coriander. It is a tasty match for the smokiness of mezcal. If you are serving this at a party, you can scale up the lime juice, mezcal, hot sauce, and Worcestershire and mix them in a pitcher and set it out for guests to add to their beer according to their own taste.

MAKES about 8 teaspoons spice mix, enough for about 12 drinks

COMPOUND gamma-terpinene

AROMAS bitter, citrus, gasoline, resin

2 tablespoons kosher salt SALT

1 teaspoon chili powder SPICY

1 teaspoon freshly ground coriander seeds

1 lime wedge SOUR

FOR EACH COCKTAIL

1 ounce (2 tablespoons) fresh lime juice SOUR

1/2 ounce (1 tablespoon) mezcal

2 teaspoons Mexican-style hot sauce (such as Cholula or Tapatio) SPICY

2 dashes Worcestershire sauce UMAMI

One 12-ounce bottle light Mexican-style beer BITTER

Combine the salt, chili powder, and coriander in a small, shallow dish and mix well. Rub the rim of a pint glass with a lime wedge, then dip the rim of the glass into the seasoning mixture.

For 1 drink, pour the lime juice, mezcal, hot sauce, and Worcestershire sauce into the glass. Fill the glass with ice and slowly pour in the beer. Serve immediately.

GRAPEFRUIT ROSEMARY SPRITZ

grapefruit, gin, aperol

We don't mind digging into chemistry a little when it produces crisp and refreshing cocktails like this. Myrcene is a compound present in all citrus and has the aroma of geranium and herb. However, myrcene is especially prominent in grapefruit, making it the perfect match for the herbaceous and floral aromas in gin, Aperol, and rosemary. (Myrcene also contributes to the pairing of grapefruit and sage, making this drink the perfect pairing for the pork recipe on page 133.)

MAKES 1 cocktail

COMPOUND
myrcene

AROMAS
geranium,
herbaceous

1 ounce (2 tablespoons) gin

1 ounce (2 tablespoons) Aperol
BITTER, SWEET

3 or 4 leaves fresh rosemary, plus a branch for garnish

½ slice pink grapefruit, plus ¼ slice for garnish SOUR, SWEET

2 ounces (¼ cup) pink grapefruit juice SOUR, SWEET

Club soda, for serving

Combine the gin, Aperol, rosemary, and grapefruit half-slice in a cocktail shaker. Muddle thoroughly. Fill the shaker with ice, then add the grapefruit juice. Shake vigorously to chill. Strain into a wine glass filled halfway with ice. Garnish with rosemary and quarter-slice grapefruit, then top with club soda.

CUCUMBER, APPLE, AND SAUVIGNON BLANC SANGRIA

cucumber, sauvignon blanc wine, grapes, apple

This recipe and the one that follows were designed specifically around the aromas naturally found in each wine—sauvignon blanc in this sangria and rosé in the one on page 192. They take advantage of the fact that vodka is an excellent solvent: It can strip aromas from ingredients, hold onto them, and carry them to other places. As the raw aromatic ingredients sit in the vodka, the alcohol will help pull both flavor and aroma from them.

MAKES 10 or more drinks

COMPOUND linalool oxide D

AROMAS citrus, floral, fragrant, green

16 ounces (2 cups) vodka

1 Kirby cucumber, thinly sliced (but not peeled)

1 cup halved seedless green grapes SWEET

1 Granny Smith apple, diced SOUR, SWEET

Sauvignon blanc wine ACID

Club soda, for serving

Combine the vodka, cucumber, grapes, and apple in a glass pitcher or jar, cover, and refrigerate at least overnight or for up to 7 days.

Strain the fruit and cucumber from the vodka. Keep the vodka in an airtight jar or bottle in the refrigerator or freezer. The fruits can be frozen to use for garnish.

To serve, mix the vodka with the wine in a one-to-three ratio: for a single glass, 1 ounce (2 tablespoons) infused vodka, 3 ounces wine. For a pitcher, mix 1 cup of the infused vodka with one 750-milliliter bottle wine.

Garnish with some of the fruit and cucumber and top with a splash of club soda.

You can make these infusions in larger batches, but do not let the fruits sit in the vodka for more than a week or they will begin to break down.

PEACH, BASIL, AND ROSÉ SANGRIA
basil, peach, lime, rosé wine

This sangria variation makes the most of the floral aromas found in stone fruits. (Botanically, peach and all stone fruits are members of rose family.)

MAKES 10 or more drinks

COMPOUND ethyl benzoate

AROMAS chamomile, celery, fat, flower, fruit

16 ounces (2 cups) vodka

¼ cup loosely packed fresh basil leaves

1 peach, pitted and thinly sliced SWEET

Grated zest of 1 lime SOUR

Provençal rosé wine, or other dry rosé ACID

Club soda, for serving

Combine the vodka, basil, peach, and lime zest in a glass pitcher or jar, cover, and refrigerate at least overnight or for up to 7 days.

Strain the peach and basil from the vodka. Keep the vodka in an airtight jar or bottle in the refrigerator or freezer. The fruit can be frozen to use for garnish.

To serve, mix the vodka with the wine in a one-to-three ratio: for a single glass, 1 ounce (2 tablespoons) infused vodka, 3 ounces wine. For a pitcher, mix 1 cup of the infused vodka with one 750-milliliter bottle rosé.

Garnish with some of the peach and top with a splash of club soda.

You can make these infusions in larger batches, but do not let the fruits sit in the vodka for more than a week or they will begin to break down.

RASPBERRY-VANILLA SODA

vanilla, raspberry, thyme

We love to have the option of sipping on something delicious, sophisticated, and alcohol free. The pairing of raspberry and thyme is bright, fresh, and totally surprising. When making this recipe, though, be careful to not let the syrup cook at a strong boil or those fresh flavors will begin to fade.

MAKES 2 cups syrup, enough for 16 drinks

COMPOUND geraniol

AROMAS geranium, lemon zest, rose, peach

2 cups fresh raspberries SWEET

½ cup sugar SWEET

1 teaspoon vanilla extract

Grated zest and juice of 1 lemon SOUR

Leaves picked from 1 branch fresh thyme, plus small branches for garnish

Club soda, for serving

Combine the raspberries, sugar, vanilla, lemon zest and juice, and thyme leaves in a saucepot. Stir and mash with a wooden spoon to break up the berries. Place the pot over medium-low heat and bring to a simmer. Cook at a gentle simmer until the berries completely break down, 3 to 4 minutes.

Remove the pot from the heat and transfer the mixture to a fine-mesh strainer set over a bowl. Slowly stir the mixture in the strainer until all of the liquid and raspberry pulp have drained through and only the solids remain. Let the syrup cool to room temperature. Store in an airtight container in the refrigerator for up to 2 weeks.

For each drink, pour 1 ounce (2 tablespoons) of the raspberry syrup into a tall glass and fill with ice. Fill the glass halfway with club soda and stir to thoroughly combine. Fill the glass the rest of the way with soda and serve. Garnish with a fresh thyme branch and serve immediately.

GRAPEFRUIT SHRUB

grapefruit, honey, vinegar

Shrubs, also known as drinking vinegars, are an essential tool in your nonalcoholic mixology game. They are bright and crisp because the mixture is never heated. Acetic acid in the vinegar helps to break down the fruits and strip the aromatics to preserve them in the resulting syrup. Let this recipe serve as a guide for creating shrubs with other fruit and herb combinations.

MAKES about 2 cups syrup, enough for 4 to 8 drinks

COMPOUND carvacrol

AROMAS caraway, spice, thyme

2 large grapefruits SOUR

¾ cup sugar SWEET

¼ cup honey (preferably wildflower) SWEET

1 cup apple cider vinegar SOUR

Water or club soda, for serving

Remove the zest from the grapefruit in large strips using a vegetable peeler. Trim off and discard the white pith from the grapefruit, and cut the fruit into segments. Place the grapefruit segments and zest and the sugar in a bowl and gently mix. Cover the bowl and leave at room temperature for 8 to 24 hours.

Stir in the honey and vinegar, re-cover, and refrigerate for 24 hours more. Remove from the refrigerator and stir until the sugar dissolves.

Strain the mixture through a fine-mesh strainer into a bowl. Discard the zest. Store the syrup in an airtight container in the refrigerator for up to 6 months.

Serve the shrub syrup as is, or dilute it with water or club soda.

SPICY PEACH SODA

peach, chile, ginger

The pairing between peach and jalapeño (which you also see in the salad on page 33) is the star of this recipe. However, if you want to capitalize on the fruity aromas of peppers without the spice, substitute slices of red bell pepper for the jalapeño.

MAKES about
1 cup purée,
enough for 4 drinks

COMPOUND
limonene

AROMAS
balsamic, citrus,
fragrant, fruit,
green, herb

2 ripe to slightly overripe peaches, pitted and cut into pieces SWEET

½ cup sugar SWEET

2 slices jalapeño chile SPICY

Small pinch of kosher salt SALT

2-inch piece fresh ginger, peeled and thinly sliced SPICY

Juice of 1 lime SOUR

Club soda, for serving

Combine the peaches, sugar, jalapeño, salt, ginger, and lime juice in a blender. Blend on high for 1 minute. Strain the purée through a fine-mesh strainer and set aside. Store in an airtight container in the refrigerator for up to 3 days.

To serve, pour 2 ounces (¼ cup) of the peach purée into a tall glass and fill with ice. Fill the glass halfway with club soda and stir to thoroughly combine. Fill the glass with soda the rest of the way and serve immediately.

HOMEMADE COLA

citrus, star anise, cinnamon, mint

The flavor of your favorite cola is truly a wonder of chemistry. The mingling of complex spice and citrus aromas is perfectly balanced to create something far greater than the individual parts. Making your own cola is a bit of a process, but the results are incredible.

MAKES about 2 cups syrup, enough for 8 to 10 drinks

COMPOUND valencene

AROMAS citrus, green oil, wood

Grated zest of 2 oranges

Grated zest of 1 lemon

Grated zest of 2 limes

¼ teaspoon ground cinnamon

5 scrapes freshly grated nutmeg

1 star anise pod, crushed

1 tablespoon minced or grated fresh ginger SPICY

1 teaspoon vanilla extract

1½ cups granulated sugar SWEET

½ cup packed brown sugar SWEET

1 tablespoon loosely packed mint leaves

Club soda, for serving

Combine the orange, lemon, and lime zests, cinnamon, nutmeg, star anise, ginger, vanilla, granulated and brown sugars, and 2 cups water in a saucepot and bring to a boil. Remove the pot from heat, add the mint, and cover the pot. Set aside for 10 minutes to infuse.

Line a colander or large strainer with cheesecloth or a clean kitchen towel and place the colander in a large bowl. Slowly pour the syrup through the colander. Transfer to a clean container, cover and store in the refrigerator up to 1 month.

To serve, pour 3 to 4 tablespoons syrup into a tall glass and fill with ice. Fill the glass halfway with club soda and stir to thoroughly combine. Fill the glass the rest of the way with soda and serve immediately.

BAKED

The browning that happens with amino acid and sugar breakdown under heat, also known as the Maillard reaction, is one of the most surefire ways to make food highly craveable. It's the reason that grocery stores vent their bakery facilities at the front door. The smell of fresh-baked anything can instantly induce hunger and get salivary glands flowing. Whether your baking is savory or sweet, your results will be determined by three main factors: gluten, moisture, and leavening. To consistently get the best results it's important to understand these elements.

Gluten

Much has been made of gluten recently. We will not get into anything health related; rather, our interest is in its function in baked goods, which is structure. Think of gluten as scaffolding, a rigid structure that forms around air bubbles. Gluten is a protein naturally found in wheat and other grains. When the gluten protein bonds with water—a process called hydration—it becomes elastic. This process happens quickly when a dough is mixed or kneaded. However, mixing is not required for gluten development. Water, on the other hand, is. You could mix a bowl full of dry flour for days on end and gluten would never develop—until water is added. Water causes gluten to develop; mixing speeds things up. The more gluten in a mixture, the denser and chewier the finished item will be. In breads, gluten is desirable; in cakes it is less so. In other words, mix bread a lot, mix cakes as little as possible.

Moisture

Moisture is one of the trickier elements in baked goods. It is essential to form gluten and allow the elements of a dough or batter to come together. However, too much moisture will prevent the structure of gluten from properly forming and the baked good will collapse. On the other hand, too little moisture will produce a dry, pasty, or mealy result. This is why accurate measuring is so important. All quality recipes are carefully formulated to have the right amount of moisture and mixing for ideal gluten development.

It is also important to note that there are certain ingredients that can help baked goods retain moisture without interfering with structure. Chief among these is sugar, which will bond with water and prevent it from evaporating. This is the reason that you will find many commercial baked goods to have high amounts of sugar: It helps ensure that the item will not dry out even after days or weeks on a shelf. Fruit and vegetable purées can also help retain moisture in baked goods, as the fiber in these bonds with and holds water in the same way that sugar can.

Leavening

This is the term bakers use for describing how air gets into an item. The most common kitchen leaveners are yeast, baking soda, and baking powder. Here's how they work.

Yeast are microorganisms that digest the sugars present in a dough and release carbon dioxide and ethanol. Yeast is slower-acting than chemical leaveners (baking soda and baking powder), typically requiring three hours or more for optimal results. Yeast also produces a unique flavor in baked goods, while chemical leaveners are flavor-neutral. Yeast is a living organism and therefore requires moisture, and is sensitive to pH; it cannot survive in an environment that is too acidic or basic.

Yeast does not have to be mixed with liquid before using, though it is typically a good idea to do so to make sure that the yeast is active. When mixed with water, active yeast should produce a foam on the surface within about 5 minutes.

Baking soda (aka sodium bicarbonate) is a chemical leavener that produces gas when it comes in contact with a liquid acid. Most people are familiar with this process from their grade school experiments in volcano making. The process is no different in baked goods: a liquid acid—buttermilk, yogurt, lemon juice, etc.—meets basic baking soda in a batter, which immediately releases gas to lighten the batter. Once all the chemicals have reacted, no more gas will be released. This means that if a baking soda–leavened batter sits too long before being baked, it will fall flat.

Baking powder works in a similar way. It is a mixture of baking soda and cream of tartar, an acid in powder form. Since both elements are present in powdered form, it will react with any liquid (not just an acid) to produce the leavening reaction. Double-acting baking powder (the most common kind) produces a second reaction when exposed to heat.

WALNUT AND OLIVE FOCACCIA

olives, walnuts, rosemary

Focaccia is a staple in our restaurant, Angelena's. We bake about a dozen loaves of plain focaccia a day just for our bread service, not to mention what we go through for sandwiches. This recipe has a few special additions of olives, walnuts, and rosemary; all three ingredients have particularly strong pairings with the aroma of baked wheat.

SERVES 6 or more

COMPOUND
pentanal

AROMAS
almond, bitter, malt, oil, pungent

1½ cups warm water

1½ teaspoons active dry yeast

18 ounces (about 3½ cups) "00" flour or bread flour

2 teaspoons sugar or honey

1 teaspoon kosher salt SALT

½ cup niçoise or kalamata olives, pitted and coarsely chopped (salt, umami, bitter)

½ cup walnut pieces (fat, bitter)

3 tablespoons olive oil FAT

1 teaspoon coarse sea salt or additional kosher salt SALT

1 tablespoon chopped fresh rosemary leaves

Whisk together the water, yeast, and sugar and set aside for 5 minutes. The mixture should become foamy. Combine the flour and kosher salt in the bowl of an electric mixer fitted with a paddle attachment. With the mixer running, pour in the water mixture. Mix until a rough dough forms. Switch the mixer attachment to the dough hook and continue to mix until the ball of dough that forms is smooth and clings to the dough hook, about 5 minutes. Add the olives and walnuts and mix for 1 minute more to incorporate them throughout the dough.

To make the dough without an electric mixer, combine the mix the water, yeast and sugar as above. Combine the flour and salt in a large mixing bowl and mix with a wooden spoon or spatula while gradually adding the water mixture until a ball of dough forms. It will be a bit of a shaggy mess at first. Knead the dough in the bowl by hand until a smooth ball forms. Add the olives and walnuts and continue kneading to incorporate them.

Transfer the dough to a lightly oiled bowl and cover with plastic wrap. Set aside at room temperature for 1 hour to proof; it should increase in size by at least half.

If the yeast does not become foamy, it is dead and your bread will not rise. Discard the yeast and try again with fresh yeast.

Spread the olive oil evenly in a 13 x 9-inch baking pan. Gently turn the dough out of the bowl into the pan. Dip your fingertips in the oil in the pan and gently press the dough out toward the corners. Cover the pan and set aside at room temperature for a minimum of 1 hour, or up to 2½ hours, until risen again and puffy. Or at this point, you can refrigerate the dough to bake it the next day. (If baking refrigerated dough, bring the dough to room temperature for 30 minutes first.)

When you're ready to bake, preheat the oven to 425°F.

Uncover the pan and gently press out the dough using just your fingertips until it fills the pan completely. Scatter the coarse salt and rosemary on the top of the bread. Bake for about 20 minutes, until the bread has risen and is well browned.

Let cool in the pan on a wire rack for 5 minutes, then remove the bread from the pan using a large metal spatula. Serve immediately or let cool directly on the rack.

CHERRY TOMATO AND NECTARINE CROSTATA

cherry tomato, nectarine, balsamic vinegar, mint

Crostata is a typically Italian dessert, a free-form tart made with whatever fruit is ripe and bountiful. We like to give it a savory twist, however. This recipe's beauty is in its versatility. Served with a salad, it is the perfect appetizer; topped with a dollop of sweetened whipped cream, it can be a great dessert.

SERVES 6 or more

COMPOUND
beta-damascenone

AROMAS
cooked apple, floral, fruit, honey, tea

CROSTATA DOUGH

12 ounces (about 2½ cups) all-purpose flour, plus more for rolling

¼ cup granulated sugar SWEET

1 teaspoon baking powder

½ teaspoon kosher salt SALT

8 tablespoons (1 stick) cold unsalted butter, cut into cubes FAT

3 large eggs FAT, UMAMI

FILLING

2 nectarines or peaches, pitted and sliced ½ inch thick SWEET

2 cups halved cherry tomatoes SWEET, UMAMI

1 tablespoon balsamic vinegar, plus more for garnish SOUR, SWEET

1 tablespoon torn fresh mint leaves, plus whole leaves for garnish

Make the dough: Combine the flour, sugar, baking powder, salt, and butter in a food processor. Run the machine in 3-second bursts until the butter is cut into small bits (about pea-size).

Separate one of the eggs and set aside the white. Beat the yolk with the remaining 2 whole eggs. Add the beaten eggs to the flour mixture and process again in short bursts until a ball begins to form. It should still be broken and uneven.

Turn the mixture out onto a work surface and gently squeeze it together to form a ball. Press it into a thin disk and wrap tightly in plastic wrap. Refrigerate for at least 30 minutes, or up to 48 hours, before rolling.

When you're ready to bake, preheat the oven to 350°F.

Make the filling: Combine the nectarines, tomatoes, balsamic vinegar, mint, sugar, and salt in a large bowl. Gently mix with a spatula. When it's well mixed, sprinkle the cornstarch over the fruit mixture and continue mixing until it has been absorbed.

Clear a large area on your work surface for rolling out the dough and lightly flour the surface. Or cover the work surface with a large piece of parchment paper and lightly flour it. Place the

continued

1 teaspoon sugar SWEET

1 teaspoon kosher salt SALT

2 tablespoons cornstarch

2 tablespoons sliced almonds
FAT

dough disk in the center and roll it out into a large circle; it should be ¼ to ½ inch thick and 18 to 20 inches in diameter.

If the dough is not yet on a piece of parchment paper, carefully transfer it to one. Brush the entire surface of the dough with the reserved egg white. Using a slotted spoon, pile the filling in the center of the dough, making sure to maintain a 3- to 4-inch border of dough around the filling on all sides. Set aside the remaining juices in the bowl.

When all of the filling has been added, fold one side the uncovered dough over to partially cover it, then rotate the crostata and fold another side. Repeat until all of the dough has been folded up around the edge and there is a large area of exposed filling in the center of the tart.

Transfer the crostata, on the parchment paper, to a baking sheet. Pour the reserved juices into the center of the filling. Brush the surface of the dough with egg white and sprinkle with the almonds. Bake for about 45 minutes, until the crust is golden brown and firm.

Cool for at least 20 minutes before cutting, though this tart is also excellent at room temperature or just slightly warm.

Always roll from the center of the dough out toward the edge. It is best to always roll in one direction, then lift and rotate the dough, rather than turning the rolling pin. If the dough is sticking to the surface as you roll, add more flour in small increments or roll the dough on lightly floured parchment paper.

NUTTY BETTER COOKIES

peanuts, fish sauce, cayenne

One day after a demo of recipes from our book *The Flavor Matrix,* Jamie found himself with loads of leftover Spicy Fish Sauce Peanut Brittle. So he decided to grind it all up until it was basically sugar again. He then used that sugar to make the most mind-blowingly unique chocolate chip cookies we had ever tasted. The fish sauce was imperceptible, but lent this incredible umami and savoriness that was the perfect counterpoint to the chocolate chip cookies, while the cooked sugar made the cookies extra chewy. This is a simplified version that still makes good use of that accidental discovery.

MAKES about 4 dozen cookies

COMPOUND guaiacol

AROMAS burnt, medicinal, phenol, smoke, wood

1 cup packed brown sugar SWEET

½ cup granulated sugar SWEET

½ cup roasted, salted peanuts FAT, SALT

2 teaspoons fish sauce or soy sauce SALT, UMAMI

¹⁄₁₆ teaspoon cayenne pepper SPICY

½ pound (2 sticks) unsalted butter, softened FAT

2 large eggs FAT

1 teaspoon vanilla extract

2¼ cups all-purpose flour

2 teaspoons baking powder

2 cups bittersweet chocolate chips BITTER, SWEET

Combine the brown sugar, granulated sugar, peanuts, fish sauce, and cayenne in a food processor and pulse in short bursts until finely chopped and well combined. Transfer the brown sugar mixture to a large bowl. Add the butter and beat with an electric mixer until light and fluffy. Beat in the eggs one at a time, fully incorporating the first one before adding the next. Beat in the vanilla. Add the flour and baking powder and beat gently until just incorporated. Stir in the chocolate chips.

Lay a large sheet of plastic wrap on a clean work surface. Transfer the cookie dough to the plastic wrap and wrap tightly, squeezing out as much air as possible. Refrigerate the dough overnight before baking.

Preheat the oven to 375°F. Line two baking sheets with parchment paper.

Scoop the chilled dough with a tablespoon measure and place on the prepared baking sheets. Flatten the scoops slightly. Bake for about 10 minutes, until golden brown at the edges. Let cool on the baking sheets for 5 minutes, then transfer the cookies to wire racks to cool completely. Store in an airtight container at room temperature for up to 2 weeks.

You don't need to actually measure the cayenne, just know that it is the tiniest possible pinch! (You can always add more.)

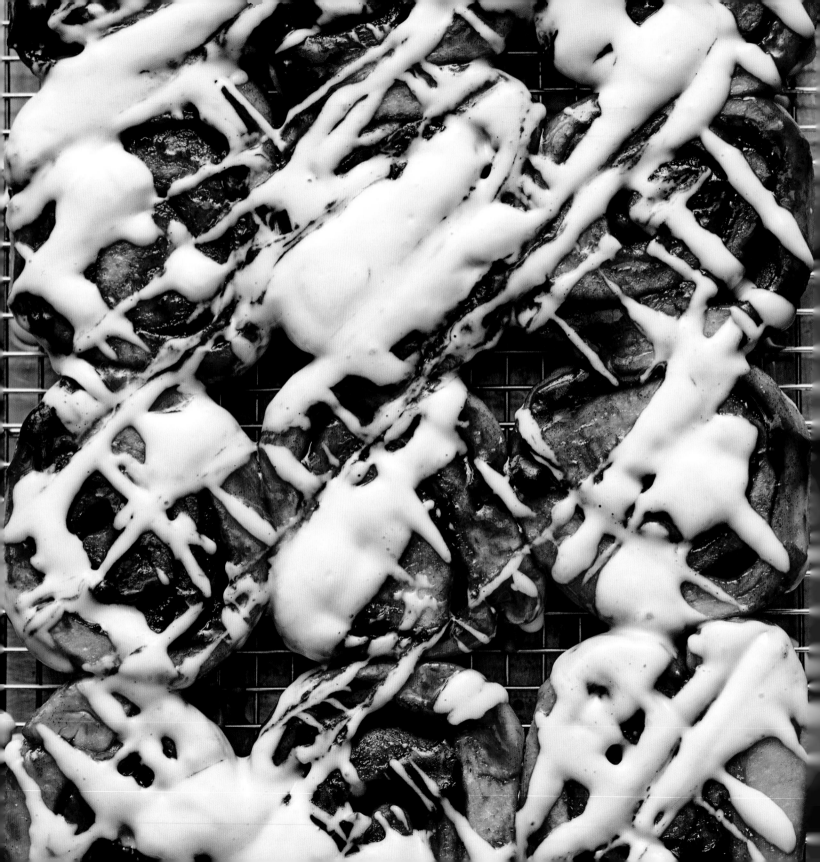

BOURBON, PECAN, AND COFFEE SWEET ROLLS

bourbon, pecans, coffee

There are some ingredients that were just meant to go together. Here, bourbon, pecans, and coffee all boast loads of rich roasted and toasted aromas, plus the triple-threat taste combo of salty, sweet, and buttery. They're like a morning on Bourbon Street in New Orleans (but without the hangover).

MAKES about 18 rolls

COMPOUND diacetylformoin

AROMAS caramel, toasted almond, butter

ROLLS

1 cup milk FAT

One ¼-ounce package active dry yeast (2¼ teaspoons)

4 tablespoons granulated sugar SWEET

3½ cups all-purpose flour, plus more for kneading

1 teaspoon kosher salt SALT

1 large egg, lightly beaten

6 tablespoons (¾ stick) unsalted butter, melted FAT

1 cup packed brown sugar SWEET

½ cup chopped pecans FAT

2 tablespoons bourbon

1 tablespoon ground cinnamon

2 teaspoons ground coffee

Make the rolls: In a small bowl, whisk together the milk, yeast, and 1 tablespoon of the granulated sugar. Set aside for about 5 minutes, until lightly foamed on the surface.

In the bowl of an electric mixer fitted with a dough hook or in a large mixing bowl, combine the flour, the remaining 3 tablespoons granulated sugar, and the salt. Mix well.

Whisk the egg and 4 tablespoons of the melted butter into the yeast mixture. Stir the yeast mixture into the dry ingredients and mix with the dough hook, or by hand with a wooden spoon, until a rough dough forms, about 5 minutes.

Turn the dough out onto a lightly floured surface and knead until smooth. Lightly oil the bowl and return the dough to it, cover with plastic wrap, and set aside for about 30 minutes; the dough should rise by approximately half.

In a small bowl, whisk together the remaining 2 tablespoons melted butter, the brown sugar, pecans, bourbon, cinnamon, and coffee until thoroughly combined.

Turn the risen dough out onto a floured surface and roll it into a rectangle about 18 x 11 inches. Scatter the brown sugar mixture evenly over the dough, gently pressing to help it hold in place.

continued

BITTER

ICING

¹/₂ cup sour cream FAT, SOUR

1 teaspoon vanilla extract

1 cup powdered sugar SWEET

Roll the dough along the long side like a jelly roll and pinch the seam together. Transfer the dough to a parchment paper–lined baking sheet and freeze for about 15 minutes, for easier cutting. Slice the roll crosswise into 1-inch pieces; you should have 18 pieces. Arrange the cut pieces in a single layer in a 13 x 9-inch baking pan. Cover the pan and let the rolls rise for about 30 minutes at room temperature, until the exterior feels puffy and springs back to a light touch. Or refrigerate, covered, overnight and bake the next morning.

When you're ready to bake, preheat the oven to 350°F.

Bake the rolls for 20 minutes, or until lightly browned.

Let the rolls cool in the pan on a wire rack for 5 minutes. Turn the rolls out onto the rack and cool for 5 minutes more.

Meanwhile, in a small bowl, whisk together the sour cream, vanilla, and powdered sugar until smooth. Spoon the glaze over the warm cinnamon rolls and serve immediately.

You can make the glaze a day in advance. Cover the bowl and store in the refrigerator. Stir to loosen it before using.

TROPICAL CARAMEL UPSIDE-DOWN CAKE

citrus, banana, pineapple, caramel

Butter, brown sugar, rum, and tropical fruits together are really a no-brainer. Pineapple upside-down cake is a classic; so are Bananas Foster. So we got to thinking that these two things would taste pretty darn good if we put them together. Boy, were we right!

SERVES 10

COMPOUND
furaneol

AROMAS
burnt, caramel, cotton candy, honey, sweet, toasted

4 tablespoons (½ stick) unsalted butter FAT

½ cup packed light brown sugar SWEET

2 tablespoons dark rum SWEET

1 cup chopped fresh pineapple, 1-inch pieces SWEET

1 banana, sliced ¾ inch thick SWEET

3 large eggs, separated

1 cup granulated sugar SWEET

1 teaspoon vanilla extract

Finely grated zest and juice of 1 orange

1 cup all-purpose flour

1 teaspoon baking powder

¼ teaspoon kosher salt SALT

Preheat the oven to 375°F.

Combine the butter, brown sugar, and rum in an oven-safe 10-inch nonstick sauté pan. Bring the mixture to a simmer over medium heat, stirring often. When the mixture is smooth and bubbling, add the pineapple and banana and stir gently to coat. Remove the pan from the heat and set aside while you make the cake batter.

Beat the egg yolks and ½ cup of the granulated sugar in a large bowl with an electric mixer until light, fluffy, and doubled in volume. While still mixing, add the vanilla, orange zest, and juice.

In a separate bowl, mix together the flour, baking powder, and salt. Add to the egg yolk mixture and beat to combine.

Beat the egg whites in a clean bowl with an electric mixer with clean beaters. When very soft peaks begin to form, slowly pour in the remaining ½ cup sugar while still beating. Continue beating until smooth, glossy peaks form. Fold the egg whites into the cake batter.

Pour the batter over the fruit-sugar mixture in the pan and smooth with a spatula. Bake for about 30 minutes, until a toothpick inserted in the center comes out clean. Cool in the pan on a wire rack for 5 minutes before inverting onto a serving plate; serve warm or at room temperature. Store any leftovers on a plate covered with plastic wrap in the refrigerator for up to 7 days.

SWEET-AND-SOUR PLUM UPSIDE-DOWN CAKE

orange, honey, vinegar, cornmeal

The only thing better than one upside-down cake (check out the one on page 213) is . . . two upside-down cakes. This one brings in some unexpected flavors that tamp down the sweetness and give this a cake a slightly savory edge. Plums and fennel are an incredible pairing, one we just can't get enough of, so even though the fennel seeds are optional, we highly recommend them.

SERVES 10

COMPOUND
gamma-decalactone

AROMAS
apricot, fat, peach, pleasant, sweet

4 tablespoons (½ stick) unsalted butter, plus more greasing the pan FAT

½ cup honey SWEET

2 tablespoons red wine vinegar SOUR

1 teaspoon fennel seeds (optional)

2 plums, pitted, each cut into 8 wedges SWEET

3 large eggs, separated

1 cup sugar SWEET

1 teaspoon vanilla extract

Finely grated zest and juice of 1 orange SWEET

¾ cup all-purpose flour

¼ cup yellow cornmeal

1 teaspoon baking powder

¼ teaspoon kosher salt SALT

Preheat the oven to 375°F. Butter a 9-inch cake pan and set aside.

Combine the butter, honey, vinegar, and fennel seeds (if using) in a large nonstick sauté pan. Bring the mixture to a simmer over medium heat, stirring often. When the mixture is smooth and bubbling, add the plums and stir gently to coat. Remove the pan from the heat and let cool slightly.

Arrange the plums in the base of prepared pan. Pour the remaining honey syrup over them, making sure that it reaches all edges of the pan. Set the pan aside while you make the cake batter.

Beat the egg yolks and ½ cup of the sugar in a large bowl with an electric mixer until light, fluffy, and doubled in volume. While still mixing, add the vanilla, orange zest, and juice.

In a separate bowl, mix together the flour, cornmeal, baking powder, and salt. Add to the egg yolk mixture and beat to combine.

Beat the egg whites in a clean bowl with an electric mixer with clean beaters. When very soft peaks begin to form, slowly pour in the remaining ½ cup sugar while still beating. Continue beating until smooth, glossy peaks form. Fold the egg whites into the cake batter.

Pour the batter over the plums and smooth with a spatula. Bake for about 30 minutes, until a toothpick inserted in the center comes out clean.

Let cool in the pan on a wire rack for 5 minutes before inverting onto serving plate. Serve warm or at room temperature. Store any leftovers on a plate covered with plastic wrap in the refrigerator for up to 7 days.

SPICY CHOCOLATE CRINKLE COOKIES

chile, coffee, cocoa

We're both suckers for spicy and sweet combos. But these go beyond that simple pleasure. Fruity aromas are secondary in peppers, cocoa, and coffee, but when they come together the flavors explode. Feel free to add as much or as little ancho powder as you like.

MAKES 2 dozen cookies

COMPOUND 2,3-butanediol

AROMAS cream, floral, fruit, herb

1 cup all-purpose flour

1/2 cup unsweetened cocoa powder BITTER

1 teaspoon baking powder

1 teaspoon ancho chile powder SPICY

1/4 teaspoon kosher salt SALT

1 cup granulated sugar SWEET

1/4 cup vegetable oil or coconut oil FAT

2 large eggs

2 teaspoons vanilla extract

1 cup powdered sugar, for coating the cookies SWEET

1 tablespoon espresso powder BITTER

Combine the flour, cocoa, baking powder, chile powder, and salt in a bowl and whisk to combine.

In a separate bowl, combine the granulated sugar and oil. Beat vigorously with a whisk or electric mixer to thoroughly combine. Add the eggs and vanilla and beat until incorporated. Continue mixing gently and add the flour mixture one-third at a time, incorporating each addition before adding the next. With the final addition of flour, the dough should form a firm ball. Remove the dough from the bowl, press it into a disk, and wrap tightly in plastic wrap. Refrigerate for at least 2 hours, ideally overnight.

When you're ready to bake, preheat the oven to 350°F. Line a baking sheet with parchment paper.

Combine the powdered sugar and espresso powder in a bowl and whisk to combine. Use a tablespoon measure to scoop the dough, making large, rounded scoops about 2 tablespoons in size. Roll each scoop between your palms to make a ball. Roll each ball in the powdered sugar mixture, then place it on the prepared baking sheet. Press each ball to partially flatten.

Bake for about 10 minutes, until the cookies are well risen and cracked on the tops.

Cool the cookies for 2 to 3 minutes on the pan, then transfer to a wire rack to cool completely. Store in an airtight container at room temperature, or in the refrigerator for up to 2 weeks.

"LIME AND THE COCONUT" POPCORN MOUSSE

popcorn, coconut, lime

Popcorn milk is an ingredient and a recipe that Jamie has been obsessed with for quite some time. He's made popcorn gelato with peanut butter swirls, popcorn crème brûlée, and even a savory popcorn cream to add an elegant finishing touch to puréed corn soup. But this popcorn mousse is probably the easiest . . . and most fun to eat of all of them. Coconut, lime, and corn are an extraordinary combination that capitalizes on the strong aromas shared by all three.

SERVES 6 or more

COMPOUND
ethyl acetate

AROMAS
brandy, contact glue, grape, sweet

MOUSSE

1 tablespoon powdered gelatin

4 tablespoons (½ stick) unsalted butter FAT

8 cups popped popcorn

2 cups milk FAT

1 cup granulated sugar SWEET

1 tablespoon vanilla extract

1 teaspoon kosher salt SALT

1 cup heavy cream FAT

1 cup powdered sugar SWEET

Make the mousse: Mix the gelatin with 2 tablespoons water in a small bowl. Set aside for 10 minutes to hydrate.

Melt the butter in a large saucepot over medium heat. Add the popcorn and stir well to coat. Cook for 3 to 5 minutes, until the popcorn is lightly toasted. Pour in the milk, sugar, vanilla, and salt. Bring to a boil, stirring often. Reduce the heat and simmer for 3 minutes, to allow the flavors to develop. Whisk in the gelatin, stirring to completely dissolve. Remove from the heat and set aside for 15 to 20 minutes to infuse the milk.

In a large bowl, combine the cream and powdered sugar. Whisk or beat on high speed with an electric mixer until stiff peaks form. Cover and refrigerate.

Strain the milk through a fine-mesh strainer into a clean glass or metal bowl. Press the popcorn with the back of a wooden spoon to extract as much liquid as possible. Discard the pressed popcorn bits. Place the milk in the refrigerator until it begins to set, whisking occasionally. Or set the bowl over another

continued

POPCORN TOPPING

2 cups popped popcorn

2 tablespoons unsalted butter, melted FAT

½ teaspoon fine sea salt SALT

¼ cup sweetened coconut flakes SWEET

1 lime

Pure chile powder or chile seasoning (such as Tajín; optional) SPICY

bowl half-filled with ice water and whisk the milk until chilled. Let the chilled milk remain over the ice for 5 to 10 minutes to begin to set.

Add one-third of the whipped cream to the milk and gently stir with a whisk to combine. Fold in another one-third of the cream. When completely incorporated, add the final third and gently fold to combine. Divide between serving dishes and place in the refrigerator until you're ready to serve.

Make the topping: Preheat the oven to 325°F.

Combine the popcorn, butter, salt, and coconut in a bowl and toss well to combine. Spread the mixture in an even layer on a baking sheet and toast in the oven until the coconut is lightly browned and aromatic, 4 to 6 minutes. Remove from the oven and finely grate the lime zest on top. Cool completely on the baking sheet. If not serving immediately, store in an airtight container or zip-top plastic bag at room temperature for up to 4 weeks.

Serve the mousse garnished with the popcorn topping and sprinkled with chile powder, if desired.

CARROT CAKE CRÈME BRÛLÉE

carrot, walnuts

We *love* carrot cake. But we decided it was time for a new take on the classic. Both carrots and walnuts have a strong affinity for heavy roasted and caramelized aromas, thus carrot cake crème brûlée was born.

SERVES 4

COMPOUND
maltol

AROMAS
caramel, cotton candy, malt, toasted bread, toasted nut

2 tablespoons unsalted butter FAT

1 cup peeled and thinly sliced carrots (about 2 medium carrots) SWEET

¼ teaspoon kosher salt SALT

¼ cup packed brown sugar SWEET

2 cups milk FAT

1 tablespoon walnut oil (optional) FAT

2 large eggs

2 large egg yolks

Granulated sugar, for topping SWEET

Preheat the oven to 325°F.

Melt the butter in a large saucepot over medium heat. Add the carrots and salt. Sauté, stirring often, until tender, 6 to 8 minutes.

When the carrots are tender, add the brown sugar and milk. Bring to a boil and simmer for about 5 minutes, until the carrots are completely soft. Transfer the contents to a blender and process until smooth. With the blender running, add the walnut oil (if using), the eggs, and yolks and blend until combined. Strain the mixture through a fine-mesh strainer into a liquid measuring cup or small pitcher.

Place four 6-ounce brûlée dishes or ovenproof ramekins inside a larger baking pan. Pour the custard mixture into the brûlée dishes. Fill the larger pan with water so the water comes halfway up the side of the brûlée dishes. Cover the baking pan with aluminum foil. Carefully transfer to the oven. Bake for 45 minutes, or until the center of the custard only has a slight wobble when the pan shakes.

Remove the pan from the oven, remove the foil, and let cool for 15 to 20 minutes. Transfer the brûlée dishes to the refrigerator to cool completely. Once chilled, you can wrap each brûlée dish in plastic wrap individually and refrigerate until you're ready to serve, up to 5 days.

To serve, cover the top of each brûlée with a thin layer of granulated sugar. Use a kitchen torch to burn the sugar, gently sweeping the flame over the surface of the brûlée until the sugar is bubbling and a deep amber color.

The goal here is get the carrots tender and concentrate their flavor. This is done by cooking as much of the water out of the carrots as possible. Try to avoid browning; if they begin to brown a bit, add water, 1 tablespoon at a time, to help the carrots cook without browning. When the carrots are cooked, it should be easy to crush the pieces with the back of a spoon.

If you don't have a torch, preheat the broiler. Put the brûlée dishes on a baking sheet and place them as close as possible to the heat. Check them every 10 seconds, as they can burn almost instantly. Serve immediately.

RHUBARB WITH BOURBON ZABAGLIONE

rhubarb, bourbon

Think of this dessert as strawberries and cream that spent the summer traveling through Europe and came back with an accent. (But not in an annoying way.) A compound called mesifurane plays an unexpectedly important role in the flavor of both rhubarb and strawberries, making both of them a great match for the roasted and woody aromas of bourbon, so if you can't find rhubarb at your local market, strawberries are a great substitute.

SERVES 4 to 6

COMPOUND
mesifurane

AROMAS
bread crust, butter, caramel

POACHED RHUBARB

2 stalks rhubarb SOUR

1 orange SWEET

1 cup granulated sugar SWEET

2 branches fresh mint, plus more for garnish

BOURBON ZABAGLIONE

6 large egg yolks FAT, UMAMI

¼ cup bourbon SWEET

1 tablespoon vanilla extract

¼ cup plus 2 tablespoons granulated sugar SWEET

1 cup heavy cream FAT

½ cup powdered sugar SWEET

To prepare the rhubarb: Trim 1 inch from the thick stalk bottom and ¼ inch from the top of the stalk.

Peel the stalks and cut into pieces about 4 inches long and ½ to 1 inch wide. Finely grate the zest of the orange; set aside a small amount for garnish. Juice the orange after you zest it.

In a wide-bottomed saucepot, bring 2 cups water and the granulated sugar to a boil. Reduce the heat to a simmer and add 2 teaspoons orange zest, the juice, mint, and rhubarb. Gently simmer until the rhubarb pieces are tender through and easily pierced with the tip of a knife, 3 to 5 minutes. Remove the pot from the heat and let the rhubarb cool in the syrup. If you're serving it within 6 hours, set aside at room temperature. Transfer to an airtight container and store in the refrigerator if holding longer, up to 2 weeks.

Make the zabaglione: Set a pot of water on the stove and bring to a simmer. Fill a large bowl about halfway with ice and water.

Combine the egg yolks, bourbon, vanilla, and granulated sugar in a heatproof bowl large enough to sit over the top of the pot

continued

You are just trimming away the dry, tough ends from the rhubarb. Larger stalks may have very woody stalks that require more trimming. The knife should trim the end fairly easily; if it is tough to cut or very fibrous, cut away more.

without touching the water. Whisk to combine, or beat with an electric mixer.

Set the bowl over the simmering water and continue whisking vigorously or beating on low speed for 6 to 8 minutes, until thick ribbons form and the mixture begins to hold soft peaks.

Remove the bowl from the pot and set it in the ice bath. Continue whisking or beating until chilled, about 5 minutes. Set aside.

Place a clean bowl over the ice, add the cream and powdered sugar, and whisk or beat until stiff peaks form. Fold the whipped cream into the cooled zabaglione. Store, covered, in the refrigerator until you're ready to serve, up to 48 hours.

To serve, divide the rhubarb between serving bowls. Spoon the zabaglione over the rhubarb and garnish with the remaining orange zest and mint.

This is the same process as for the first stage of making hollandaise. Because it has much more liquid mixed with the eggs than hollandaise would, it will take longer for them to reach the ribbon stage. It's important to have patience. The eggs yolks must be gently cooked to just the right doneness—if overcooked, they will curdle, and if undercooked, the zabaglione will be soupy and loose.

———

Save the rhubarb syrup. It's great for cocktails (particularly with gin and bourbon), or can be mixed with club soda for a refreshing non-alcoholic drink.

NOT-THAT-KIND-OF-MUSHROOM BROWNIES

mushrooms, cocoa

Mushrooms in a dessert may sound like a terrible idea, but the earthiness of mushrooms actually fades into the background and just serves to amp up the rich cocoa flavor. In *The Flavor Matrix* you can find our recipe for a porcini, hazelnut, and chocolate torte, which makes an elegant dessert, but these fudgy brownies are unique and snackable.

MAKES about 24 brownies

COMPOUND
3-octanol

AROMAS
citrus, moss, mushroom, nut, oil

4 large eggs

1 cup Dutch-process unsweetened cocoa powder BITTER

1 tablespoon mushroom powder (porcini is best) UMAMI

1 teaspoon kosher salt SALT

1 teaspoon baking powder

1 tablespoon vanilla extract

¹⁄₂ pound (2 sticks) unsalted butter FAT

2 cups granulated sugar SWEET

¹⁄₄ cup packed light brown sugar SWEET

1¹⁄₂ cups whole wheat flour or all-purpose flour

2 cups semisweet chocolate chips BITTER, SWEET

Preheat the oven to 350°F. Grease a 13 x 9-inch baking pan.

In a large bowl, combine the eggs, cocoa, mushroom powder, salt, baking powder, and vanilla. Whisk or beat with an electric mixer until smooth.

Combine the butter, granulated sugar, and brown sugar in a saucepot over medium heat and cook, stirring, until the butter is melted and the sugars have dissolved.

Remove the pot from the heat and add the flour and chocolate chips. Whisk until smooth.

Pour the chocolate-butter mixture into the egg mixture and beat again until smooth. Transfer the batter to the prepared pan and smooth the top with a spatula. Bake for 30 minutes, or until a toothpick inserted into the center of the pan comes out clean.

Let cool completely in the pan on a wire rack before cutting. Store in an airtight container in the refrigerator for up to 10 days.

Melting the butter and sugar together will help produce a shiny crust on top of the baked brownies.

"THE KING" OF BROWNIES

peanut butter, banana, chocolate

The flavors here are familiar—it's the technique that makes these brownies amazing. Bananas and peanut butter work double duty as they not only make the brownies taste great, but also make them impossibly gooey and rich-tasting without overloading on fat and sugar. We think Elvis would have approved.

MAKES about 16 brownies

COMPOUND 3-hydroxy-2-methyl-4-pyrone

AROMAS caramel, cotton candy, malt, toasted bread, toasted nut

2 ripe bananas SWEET

1 large egg

1 cup packed light brown sugar SWEET

1 teaspoon vanilla extract

8 tablespoons (1 stick) unsalted butter FAT

2 cups bittersweet chocolate chips BITTER, SWEET

¾ cup all-purpose flour

¼ cup unsweetened cocoa powder BITTER

½ cup creamy peanut butter (fat, sweet)

Preheat the oven to 350°F. Grease a 9 x 9-inch baking pan.

Combine the bananas, egg, ½ cup of the brown sugar, and the vanilla in a bowl and beat with an electric mixer until smooth.

Combine the remaining ½ cup brown sugar and the butter in a small saucepot. Cook over medium heat, stirring often, until the sugar has melted. Remove from the heat, add the chocolate chips, and stir until smooth. Beat the butter-chocolate mixture into the banana mixture. Add the flour and cocoa and stir to combine. Transfer the batter to the prepared pan. Drop spoonfuls of the peanut butter over the top of the batter and swirl with the back of a spoon.

Bake for about 25 minutes, until the edges are set and a toothpick inserted into the center comes out slightly wet.

Let cool completely in the pan on a wire rack before cutting into squares. Store in an airtight container, or tightly wrapped, in the refrigerator for up to 10 days.

Brown Butter

The next three recipes incorporate brown butter. Making brown butter is one of the simplest things you can do in your kitchen to amp up roasted, nutty aromas in food. These are particularly desirable in desserts, where the aromas pair particularly well with vanilla, and generally enhance flavor. Always use unsalted butter for brown butter.

Brown butter is made by toasting the milk solids present in whole butter. To do this, you must first melt the butter and boil out all of the water it contains (a process known as clarifying). Once the butter is clarified, you will see the milk solids collected at the bottom. Reduce the heat under the pot and watch carefully as the solids begin to toast. The amount of toastiness is up to you: When the solids have a light amber color, the butter will have a very delicate flavor; it will become more nutty and robust as it darkens further. Also note that the butter will continue to cook after it's removed from the heat, turning another one or two shades darker, unless you strain it immediately into a separate heatproof container. So ideally you should remove it from the heat just before it turns the desired color. At its deepest and richest, the butter will look nearly black before straining, but be careful—at this stage it quickly turns from brown butter to burnt butter.

Always let the butter cool in the pot or another heatproof container. Do not pour it directly into any plastic container—the butter is extremely hot and will melt right through the plastic.

Brown butter can be made in large batches and stored in the refrigerator or freezer indefinitely. Since most butter is 17 to 20 percent water, you should expect the quantity of brown butter to be less that you started with, so account for this when making a batch for recipes. You may substitute regular butter for any of the following recipes; however, we highly recommend taking the time to make brown butter.

BROWN BUTTER–ESPRESSO CARROT CAKE

walnuts, espresso, carrot

SERVES 10

COMPOUND
5-methylfurfural

AROMAS
almond, caramel, cooked, roasted garlic, spice

Though not necessary, whole wheat flour adds a little extra nuttiness to the cake; you could use all-purpose if you prefer.

CARROT CAKE

½ pound (2 sticks) unsalted butter FAT

3 large eggs

1 cup granulated sugar SWEET

½ cup packed brown sugar SWEET

¼ cup milk FAT

½ teaspoon kosher salt SALT

2 cups whole wheat flour

¼ cup all-purpose flour

1 teaspoon baking powder

½ teaspoon baking soda

½ teaspoon ground cinnamon

3 cups grated carrots (about 3 carrots) SWEET

1 cup chopped walnuts FAT, BITTER

CREAM CHEESE ICING

4 tablespoons (½ stick) unsalted butter, softened FAT

4 ounces cream cheese, softened FAT

½ cup powdered sugar SWEET

1 teaspoon espresso powder or ground coffee BITTER

½ teaspoon vanilla extract

Make the cake: Preheat the oven to 350°F. Grease a 9 x 5-inch loaf pan.

Brown the butter as described on page 226. Set aside to cool slightly.

Combine the eggs, granulated sugar, brown sugar, brown butter, milk, and salt. Whisk or beat with an electric mixer to combine. In a separate bowl, mix together the flours, baking powder, baking soda, and cinnamon. Add to the egg mixture and stir until just combined. Add the carrots and nuts and stir by hand to combine. Pour the batter into the prepared pan. Smooth the top with a spatula.

Bake for about 50 minutes, until a toothpick inserted into the center of the cake comes out clean. Let cool completely in the pan.

Make the icing: Combine the butter, cream cheese, sugar, espresso powder, and vanilla in a bowl and beat together with an electric mixer until smooth.

Remove the cake from the pan and place it on a plate. Spread the icing over the top in a thick layer. Store loosely covered with plastic wrap or a cake dome in the refrigerator for up to 10 days.

BROWN BUTTER ICE CREAM SUNDAE

brown butter, vanilla

Vanilla loves roasted, nutty aromas. This recipe brings a triple threat of flavor with nutty quinoa, brown butter, and caramel. Not only that—quinoa in dessert means you can tell yourself that your ice cream indulgence is healthy. Score!

SERVES 8 or more

COMPOUND
anisaldehyde

AROMAS
almond, anise, caramel, mint, sweet

8 tablespoons (1 stick) unsalted butter FAT

1 cup quinoa, rinsed and drained BITTER

½ teaspoon kosher salt SALT

2 cups sugar SWEET

2 teaspoons vanilla extract

¼ cup sesame seeds

1 teaspoon large-flake sea salt SALT

Ice cream of your choice, 2 scoops per person FAT, SWEET

Brown the butter as described on page 226 to medium brown. Set aside to cool slightly.

Bring 2 cups water to a boil. Add the quinoa and kosher salt and stir well. Cover the pot and turn the heat to low. Cook without stirring until all of the liquid has been absorbed, about 15 minutes.

Remove from the heat and spread the quinoa in a thin layer on a baking sheet to steam-dry.

Line a baking sheet with a silicone baking mat, or with parchment paper and grease the parchment with nonstick cooking spray.

In a heavy saucepot, stir together the sugar and 2 tablespoons of water. Place the pot over medium-high heat and cook, swirling the pot occasionally as the sugar melts; do not stir. If you notice crystals forming around the side of the pot, wipe the inside with a brush moistened with water to wash the crystals back into the caramel.

Continue cooking the caramel at a simmer until it is deep brown, 12 to 15 minutes.

The temperature should register between 330° and 350°F on a candy or deep-fry thermometer.

Making caramel can be a bit tricky. If any small solids get introduced to the pan, the sugar will begin to crystalize around them and ruin the caramel. This is why you should avoid stirring, and only use water to clean down the sides of the pot.

continued

As soon as the caramel is ready, reduce the heat to low and stir in the quinoa, brown butter, and vanilla. Mix gently to avoid splattering or spilling the caramel. Cook for 3 to 5 minutes more to expel any remaining moisture from the quinoa; the bubbling should mostly subside. Remove from the heat and stir in the sesame seeds.

Spread the finished caramel in a thin layer on the prepared baking sheet with a heatproof spatula. Sprinkle the sea salt over the caramel and let it cool completely. When cooled, break into pieces and store in an airtight container in the refrigerator.

To serve, scoop ice cream into bowls and crumble the brittle over the top.

It is important to make sure you cook out all of the moisture in this step or the brittle will not get crunchy. If you find your caramel is a bit soft, spreading it into a thin layer on a silicone baking mat and baking it at 325°F for 12 minutes may help eliminate the excess water. The caramel will still seem soft as soon as it comes out of the oven, but will firm upon cooling.

NUTELLA AND BROWN BUTTER SQUASH PANINI

vanilla, squash, nutella

Veggies for dessert? We say, "Why not!?" This combination is based on squash's strong affinity for roasted and nutty aromas. You can make these crazy-good sandwiches with sweet potatoes instead of squash, though we prefer the way-less-sweet taste of butternut squash. Either way, these are a completely unexpected treat that everyone is going to love.

SERVES 4 to 8

COMPOUND
2,3-pentanedione

AROMAS
bitter, butter, caramel, fruit, sweet

4 tablespoons (½ stick) unsalted butter, plus more for cooking the sandwiches FAT

½ medium butternut squash (about 2 pounds), peeled, seeded, and cut in ¼- to ½-inch slices SWEET

½ teaspoon kosher salt SALT

1 tablespoon vanilla extract

½ cup powdered sugar, plus more for serving SWEET

½ to 1 cup chocolate-hazelnut spread (such as Nutella) FAT, SWEET

8 slices white sandwich bread or cinnamon-raisin bread SWEET

Brown the 4 tablespoons butter in a large sauté pan as described on page 226. Add the butternut squash and season with the salt. Sauté, stirring often, until just tender, about 5 minutes.

Add the vanilla and powdered sugar and stir until the sugar has completely dissolved. Remove from the heat and set aside to cool.

Spread 1 to 2 tablespoons of the chocolate hazelnut spread on each slice of bread. Sandwich with the cooked squash in between to make four sandwiches.

Spread the outside of each sandwich on both sides with a thin layer of butter. Cook each sandwich in a sandwich press or non-stick sauté pan over medium heat until toasted and golden on the outside, 2 to 3 minutes per side if sautéing.

Serve the sandwiches immediately, dusted with powdered sugar.

CHOCOLATE AND RED WINE BREAD PUDDING

merlot wine, chocolate, whiskey

These are a few—well, *all*—of Brooke's favorite things. We have always enjoyed nibbling on a little dark chocolate while sipping red wine or a little bourbon at the end of a meal. It's clear why: These three ingredients are a very strong match based on their aroma profiles. They all develop similar toasted aromas, but in different ways—bourbon and wine draw them from the wooden barrels they are aged in, while cocoa beans develop them during drying and roasting. However it happens, when combined into a warm, comforting bread pudding with a creamy sauce, the result is magical.

SERVES 8 or more

COMPOUND
2-propenal

AROMAS
burnt, sweet, pungent

BREAD PUDDING

1 cup sugar SWEET

4 large eggs

¼ cup unsweetened cocoa powder BITTER

2 teaspoons vanilla extract

2 cups milk FAT

Pinch of freshly grated nutmeg

⅛ teaspoon ground cinnamon

One 12-inch loaf French bread, crusts trimmed, cut into 1-inch cubes

8 tablespoons (1 stick) unsalted butter, cut into cubes FAT

2 cups (12 ounces) chopped bittersweet chocolate BITTER, SWEET

Make the bread pudding: In a large bowl, combine the sugar, eggs, cocoa, and vanilla and whisk until smooth. Add the milk, nutmeg, and cinnamon and continue whisking to combine. Stir in the bread, mix well, and set aside for the bread to soften, about 30 minutes.

While the bread is soaking, preheat the oven to 350° F. Grease a 13 x 9-inch baking dish.

When the bread is completely softened, add the butter, chocolate, bourbon, and pistachios, if using. Stir well. Transfer the mixture to the prepared pan. Bake, uncovered, for 45 minutes, or until the center of the bread pudding is just set. The surface should be browned and firm to the touch with a bit of give. When you lightly press in the center, no liquid should rise to the surface.

Let cool in the baking dish on a wire rack for at least 15 minutes.

The bread should soak up nearly all of the custard. Occasionally stir the bowl from the bottom to evenly distribute the custard.

continued

½ cup bourbon SWEET

1 cup shelled unsalted pistachios (optional) FAT

MERLOT SAUCE

1 cup merlot wine ACID

1 cup sugar SWEET

1 cup heavy cream FAT

Make the sauce: Combine the wine and sugar in a small sauce-pot and bring to a boil. Lower the heat and simmer until reduced by half, about 8 minutes. Add the cream and cook for about 2 minutes more, until the sauce is thick and smooth.

Serve the bread pudding drizzled with a generous amount of the merlot sauce. Store any leftover bread pudding tightly wrapped in the refrigerator for up to 10 days and reheat to serve.

VERNACCIA-POACHED PEARS WITH PECORINO

vernaccia wine, pear, pecorino

When researching our book *The Flavor Matrix,* we learned that there really is something to the adage "what grows together, goes together" because many flavor-creating aromas are imprinted into foods by their environment. With these pears, we bring together the best of Tuscany: Vernaccia di San Gimignano and the Val d'Orcia's best sheeps' milk cheese, pecorino. A major compound found in vernaccia grapes is 2-phenylethanol, with its aromas of honey, lilac, and rose. Pear, being a member of the Rosaceae family, carries many of these floral aromas as well. Most impressively, this recipe is all at once salty, tart, piquant, and sweet.

SERVES 8

COMPOUND
2-phenylethanol

AROMAS
honey, lilac, rose

One 750-milliliter bottle vernaccia or other dry white wine ACID

1 cinnamon stick

2 teaspoons black peppercorns SPICY

2 teaspoons vanilla extract

2 star anise pods

1 cup sugar SWEET

Grated zest of 1 lemon

4 Bosc pears, peeled, halved, and cored SWEET

1 cup whipped cream, for serving FAT

1/2 cup finely grated pecorino cheese FAT, SALT, UMAMI

Combine the wine, cinnamon, peppercorns, vanilla, star anise, sugar, and lemon zest in a saucepot. Add the pears and enough water to cover them completely. Bring the mixture to a boil. Reduce the heat to a simmer, cover the pot, and cook until the pears are just tender to the tip of a knife, about 45 minutes.

Remove from the heat and let the pears cool slightly in the poaching liquid. The pears may be stored, covered, in the poaching liquid for up to 2 weeks.

Serve the pears with whipped cream and a generous sprinkling of pecorino.

INDEX

Note: Page references in *italics* indicate photographs.

A

Acid/sour flavors, 9
Almond-Cherry Pesto, 118
Anchovy(ies)
  Caesar Artichoke Dip, 39
  Vinaigrette, Grilled Lamb with, 146, *147*
Apple(s)
  Balsamic Vinegar, and Bourbon, Pan-Seared Pork Medallions with, *130*, 131–32
  -Brined Pork with Caramelized Onion and Bourbon Gravy, 134–35
  Crisp, and Crab Salad, 180
  Cucumber, and Sauvignon Blanc Sangria, 190, *191*
  and Ham Grilled Cheese Sandwiches, 83
Artichoke Dip, Caesar, 39
Asparagus and Potato Chip Gratin, *36*, 37–38
Avocado
  Cream and Spiced Potatoes, Fish with, 168–69
  "Succotash," *24*, 25
  Toast, 22, *23*

B

Bacon
  and Creamy Tomato Farro, Fish with, *154*, 155
  and Kiwi Grilled Cheese Sandwiches, Spicy, 80, *81*
Ultimate BLT with "To-Mayo," 84–86, *85*
Baked goods, about, 202–3
Baking powder, 203
Baking soda, 203
Bananas
  "The King" of Brownies, *224*, 225
  Tropical Caramel Upside-Down Cake, 213
Basil
  Broccoli and Pistachio Pesto, 42
  Milk-Poached Fish with, 158–59
  Peach, and Rosé Sangria, 192, *193*
  and Pineapple Relish, Spicy, Grilled Pork with, 127–28, *129*
Beef
  Chianti-Braised, with Grits, 122–25, *123*
  and Eggplant, Grilled, with Espresso Butter, 119–21, *120*
  internal cooking temperatures, 111
  Pan-Seared, with Bourbon-Raisin Sauce, 114–15
  Seared Steaks with Almond-Cherry Pesto, *116*, 117–18
  and Sweet Potato Ale Stew, Slow Cooker, 112–13
Beer
  Mezcal Michelada, 187
Beet, Roasted, Salad, *26*, 27
Bitter flavors, 11
Bourbon
  Apples, and Balsamic Vinegar, Pan-Seared Pork Medallions with, *130*, 131–32
  Chocolate and Red Wine Bread Pudding, 233–35, *234*
Gravy and Caramelized Onion, Apple-Brined Pork with, 134–35
  -Pecan and Coffee Sweet Rolls, *210*, 211–12
  -Raisin Sauce, Pan-Seared Beef with, *114*, 115–16
  Spiced Butternut Squash Old Fashioned, 186
  Zabaglione, Rhubarb with, *220*, 221–22
Bread. *See also* Toasts
  Bourbon-Pecan and Coffee Sweet Rolls, *210*, 211–12
  Pudding, Chocolate and Red Wine, 233–35, *234*
  Walnut and Olive Focaccia, 204–5
Broccoli
  and Kimchi Grilled Cheese Sandwiches, 82
  Pan-Seared Fish with, 153
  and Pistachio Pesto, 42
Broccoli Rabe
  Frico, aka Crispy Cheese Cakes, 87–89, *88*
Brownies
  Not-That-Kind-of-Mushroom, 223
  "The King" of, *224*, 225
Bruschetta
  Lump Crab, *178*, 179
  Watermelon, *30*, 31
Brussels Sprouts Kebabs, 34, *35*
Butter
  about, 7–9
  Brown, and Grape Vinaigrette, Pan-Seared Fish with, *160*, 161
  Brown, and Nutella Squash Panini, 232

Brown, Espresso Carrot Cake, *227,*
228
Brown, Ice Cream Sundae, 229–30,
231
brown, preparing, 226
Brown, Spring Vegetable, and
Lemon Pasta, 52–54, *53*
Espresso, 121

C

Cabbage
Coco-Slaw, 19
Cakes
Brown Butter Espresso Carrot, *227,*
228
Sweet-and-Sour Plum Upside-
Down, 214–15
Tropical Caramel Upside-Down, 213
Carrot(s)
Cake, Brown Butter Espresso, *227,*
228
Cake Crème Brûlée, 219
Herbed, and Mustard, Pan-Seared
Chicken with, 99
and Roast Lamb with Mint and
Lemon, 144
Soup, Chilled, with Poached Shrimp,
171–73, *172*
Squash Skewers, 44, *45*
Cauliflower
Bake, Buffalo, 75
Whole Roasted, 40, *41*
Cheese
Asparagus and Potato Chip Gratin,
36, 37–38
Blue, and Mushroom-Potato Gratin,
Braised Lamb with, 139–40
Buffalo Cauliflower Bake, 75
Caesar Artichoke Dip, 39
Cakes, Crispy, aka Frico, 87–89, *88*
Cranberry-Stuffed Baked Brie, *76,*
77–78

Farro and Crispy Kale Salad, 63–64,
65
flavor variables, 72–73
Grilled, Sandwich, Broccoli and
Kimchi, 82
Grilled, Sandwich, Spicy Kiwi and
Bacon, 80, *81*
Grilled, Sandwich, Ultimate, 79
Grilled, Sandwiches, Ham and
Apple, 83
Mac and, Creamed Kale and
Caramelized Onion, 55–56, *57*
Scalloped Parsnips, 47
Summer Squash Gratin, *48,* 49
Sweet Pea and Mushroom Rigatoni
Carbonara, 68–69
Vernaccia-Poached Pears with
Pecorino, 236, *237*
Cherry
-Almond Pesto, 118
-Olive Jam, 74
Chicken
cooking methods, 92–93
cooking temperatures, 94
Fingers, Ginger Beer–Battered, *106,*
107
and Green Vegetable Pilau, Indian,
108–9
Grilled, Salad, Southwestern, 102
Honey Mustard, Ultimate, *100,* 101
Pan-Roasted, with Creamed Greens
and Potatoes, 96–98, *97*
Pan-Seared, with Herbed Carrots
and Mustard, 99
and Pomegranate Lettuce Wraps,
Spicy, 95
Tomato Ragu, Creamy, 103–4, *105*
Chocolate
Cocoa and Lemon Old Fashioned,
185
Crinkle Cookies, Spicy, 216
Not-That-Kind-of-Mushroom
Brownies, 223

Nutella and Brown Butter Squash
Panini, 232
Nutty Better Cookies, 209
and Red Wine Bread Pudding,
233–35, *234*
"The King" of Brownies, *224,* 225
Chutney, Cranberry, 78
Clams
Summer Squash Vongole, *66,* 67
Clarified butter/ghee, 9
Coconut
Coco-Slaw, 19
"Lime and the Coconut" Popcorn
Mousse, 217–18
and Shrimp Stew, Brazilian, 176, *177*
Coffee
and Bourbon-Pecan Sweet Rolls,
210, 211–12
Brown Butter Espresso Carrot Cake,
227, 228
Espresso Butter, 121
Cookies
Nutty Better, 209
Spicy Chocolate Crinkle, 216
Corn
Avocado "Succotash," *24,* 25
Southwestern Grilled Chicken
Salad, 102
Crab
and Crisp Apple Salad, 180
Lump, Bruschetta, *178,* 179
Cranberry
Chutney, 78
-Stuffed Baked Brie, *76,* 77–78
Crème Brûlée, Carrot Cake, 219
Crostata, Cherry Tomato and Nectarine,
206, 207–8
Crustaceans. *See also* Clams; Crab;
Lobster; Shrimp
cooking methods, 170
Cucumber(s)
Apple, and Sauvignon Blanc
Sangria, 190, *191*

A Different Kind of Green Salad, 28, *29*

D

Dips
    Caesar Artichoke, 39
    Eggplant, 43
Drinks
    aromatic compounds in, 184
    Cocoa and Lemon Old Fashioned, 185
    Cucumber, Apple, and Sauvignon Blanc Sangria, 190, *191*
    Grapefruit Rosemary Spritz, *188,* 189
    Grapefruit Shrub, 196, *197*
    Homemade Cola, 199
    Mezcal Michelada, 187
    Peach, Basil, and Rosé Sangria, 192, *193*
    Raspberry-Vanilla Soda, *194,* 195
    Spiced Butternut Squash Old Fashioned, 186
    Spicy Peach Soda, 198

E

Eggplant
    and Beef, Grilled, with Espresso Butter, 119–21, *120*
    Dip, 43
Eggs
    Sweet Pea and Mushroom Rigatoni Carbonara, 68–69

F

Farro
    and Crispy Kale Salad, 63–64, *65*
    Tomato, Creamy, and Bacon, Fish with, *154,* 155
Fats, 7–9
Fennel
    -Seared Fish with Green Beans, Sesame, and Dill, *164,* 165–66

Sicilian-Style Peach Salad, *32, 33*
Fish. *See also* Anchovy(ies)
    with Bacon and Creamy Tomato Farro, *154,* 155
    broiling or grilling, 152
    cooking, 150–51
    Fennel-Seared, with Green Beans, Sesame, and Dill, *164,* 165–66
    full-flavored, 150, 151
    with Lemon-Dill Lettuce Sauté, 156, *157*
    mild-flavored, 150, 151
    Milk-Poached, with Basil, 158–59
    Miso and Maple-Glazed, 162
    Pan-Seared, with Broccoli, 153
    Pan-Seared, with Brown Butter and Grape Vinaigrette, *160,* 161
    pan-searing, 152
    with Spiced Potatoes and Avocado Cream, 168–69
    with Sweet Pea and Ham Quinoa Pilaf, 163
    with Sweet Potato Hash and Poblano, 167
Flavors
    acid/sour, 9
    bitter, 11
    fats, 7–9
    pairing principles, 6
    salt, 10
    sweet, 11
    umami, 10–11
Fruits, 16–17. *See also specific fruits*

G

Garlic
    Eggplant Dip, 43
    Umami in a Bottle, 18
Gin
    Grapefruit Rosemary Spritz, *188,* 189
Gluten, 202
Grains, 50–51. *See also specific grains*

Grapefruit
    Rosemary Spritz, *188,* 189
    Shrub, 196, *197*
Grape(s)
    and Brown Butter Vinaigrette, Pan-Seared Fish with, *160, 161*
    A Different Kind of Green Salad, 28, *29*
    Southwestern Grilled Chicken Salad, 102
Green Beans, Sesame, and Dill, Pan-Seared Fish with, *164,* 165–66
Greens. *See also specific greens*
    Creamed, and Potatoes, Pan-Roasted Chicken with, 96–98, *97*
Grits, Creamy Stone-Ground, *124,* 125

H

Ham
    and Apple Grilled Cheese Sandwiches, 83
    and Sweet Pea Quinoa Pilaf, Fish with, 163
Honey Mustard Chicken, Ultimate, *100,* 101
Horseradish and Citrus-Crusted Lamb Roast, 145

I

Ice Cream Sundae, Brown Butter, 229–30, *231*

J

Jam, Cherry-Olive, 74

K

Kale
    Creamed, and Caramelized Onion Mac and Cheese, 55–56, *57*
    Crispy, and Farro Salad, 63–64, *65*
Kimchi and Broccoli Grilled Cheese Sandwiches, 82

Kiwi and Bacon Grilled Cheese
    Sandwiches, Spicy, 80, *81*

L
Lamb
    about, 138
    Braised, with Blue Cheese and
        Mushroom-Potato Gratin, 139–
        40
    Braised, with Spicy Peach Chutney,
        141–42, *143*
    Grilled, with Anchovy Vinaigrette,
        146, *147*
    internal cooking temperatures, 111
    Roast, and Carrots with Mint and
        Lemon, 144
    Roast, Horseradish and Citrus-
        Crusted, 145
Lard, 8
Leaveners, 203
Leeks, Grilled, Vinaigrette, 20–21
Lemon
    and Cocoa Old Fashioned, 185
    Homemade Cola, 199
Lettuce
    Grilled Lamb with Anchovy
        Vinaigrette, 146, *147*
    Lemon-Dill, Sauté, Fish with, 156,
        157
    Ultimate BLT with "To-Mayo," 84–
        86, *85*
    Wraps, Spicy Pomegranate and
        Chicken, 95
"Lime and the Coconut" Popcorn
    Mousse, 217–18
Lobster, Grilled, and Butternut Squash
    with Tomato, Olive, and Preserved
    Lemon Relish, 181

M
Maillard reaction, 93
Maple and Miso-Glazed Fish, 162
Meat, 110–11. *See also* Beef; Lamb; Pork

Melon
    A Different Kind of Green Salad, 28,
        29
    Watermelon Bruschetta, *30,* 31
Mezcal Michelada, 187
Milk-Poached Fish with Basil, 158–59
Miso and Maple-Glazed Fish, 162
Mousse, "Lime and the Coconut"
    Popcorn, 217–18
Mushroom(s)
    Asparagus and Potato Chip Gratin,
        36, 37–38
    Fish with Sweet Potato Hash and
        Poblano, 167
    Grilled Leeks Vinaigrette, 20–21
    Not-That-Kind-of-Mushroom
        Brownies, 223
    "Pancetta," Rigatoni alla Gricia with,
        58, 59
    -Potato Gratin and Blue Cheese,
        Braised Lamb with, 139–40
    and Sweet Pea Rigatoni Carbonara,
        68–69
Mustard
    Honey Chicken, Ultimate, *100,* 101
    Orange, and Sage, Slow Cooker
        Pork with, 133
    Umami in a Bottle, 18

N
Nectarine and Cherry Tomato Crostata,
    206, 207–8
Nutella and Brown Butter Squash
    Panini, 232

O
Oils, 8
Olive oil, 7
Olive(s)
    -Cherry Jam, 74
    Gremolata, Vegetable Bolognese
        with, 70–71
    Sicilian-Style Peach Salad, *32,* 33

and Walnut Focaccia, 204–5
Onion(s)
    Caramelized, and Bourbon Gravy,
        Apple-Brined Pork with, 134–35
    Caramelized, and Creamed Kale
        Mac and Cheese, 55–56, *57*
Orange
    Homemade Cola, 199
    Mustard, and Sage, Slow Cooker
        Pork with, 133

P
Parsnips, Scalloped, 47
Pasta
    Creamed Kale and Caramelized
        Onion Mac and Cheese, 55–56,
        57
    Creamy Tomato Chicken Ragu,
        103–4, *105*
    Pumpkin Pilaf, 46
    Rigatoni alla Gricia with Mushroom
        "Pancetta," *58,* 59
    Shrimp, Creamy, with Charred
        Tomato and Pumpkin, 174–75
    Spring Vegetable, Brown Butter, and
        Lemon, 52–54, *53*
    Summer Squash Vongole, *66,* 67
    Sweet Pea and Mushroom Rigatoni
        Carbonara, 68–69
    Vegetable Bolognese with Olive
        Gremolata, 70–71
Peach
    Basil, and Rosé Sangria, 192, *193*
    Chutney, Spicy, Braised Lamb with,
        141–42, *143*
    Salad, Sicilian-Style, *32,* 33
    Soda, Spicy, 198
Peanut Butter
    "The King" of Brownies, *224, 225*
Peanuts
    Nutty Better Cookies, 209

Pear(s)
    Brown Butter, and Maple Pork Roast, 136–37
    Vernaccia-Poached, with Pecorino, 236, *237*
Pea(s)
    Indian Chicken and Green Vegetable Pilau, 108–9
    Spring Vegetable, Brown Butter, and Lemon Pasta, 52–54, *53*
    Sweet, and Ham Quinoa Pilaf, Fish with, 163
    Sweet, and Mushroom Rigatoni Carbonara, 68–69
Pecan-Bourbon and Coffee Sweet Rolls, *210*, 211–12
Pesto
    Almond-Cherry, 118
    Broccoli and Pistachio, 42
Pineapple
    and Basil Relish, Spicy, Grilled Pork with, 127–28, *129*
    Tropical Caramel Upside-Down Cake, 213
Pistachio and Broccoli Pesto, 42
Plum Upside-Down Cake, Sweet-and-Sour, 214–15
Pomegranate and Chicken Lettuce Wraps, Spicy, 95
Popcorn Mousse, "Lime and the Coconut," 217–18
Pork. *See also* Bacon; Ham
    about, 126
    Apple-Brined, with Caramelized Onion and Bourbon Gravy, 134–35
    Grilled, with Spicy Pineapple and Basil Relish, 127–28, *129*
    Medallions, Pan-Seared, with Apples, Balsamic Vinegar, and Bourbon, *130,* 131–32
    Roast, Brown Butter, Maple, and Pear, 136–37
    Slow Cooker, with Mustard, Orange, and Sage, 133
Potato Chip and Asparagus Gratin, *36,* 37–38
Potato(es). *See also* Sweet Potato(es)
    and Creamed Greens, Pan-Roasted Chicken with, 96–98, *97*
    Fish with Lemon-Dill Lettuce Sauté, 156, *157*
    -Mushroom Gratin and Blue Cheese, Braised Lamb with, 139–40
    Scalloped Parsnips, 47
    Spiced, and Avocado Cream, Fish with, 168–69
Pumpkin
    and Charred Tomato, Creamy Shrimp Pasta with, 174–75
    Pilaf, 46

Q

Quinoa
    Brown Butter Ice Cream Sundae, 229–30, *231*
    Pilaf, Sweet Pea and Ham, Fish with, 163
    Salad, *60,* 61–62

R

Raisin-Bourbon Sauce, Pan-Seared Beef with, *114,* 115–16
Raspberry-Vanilla Soda, *194,* 195
Rhubarb with Bourbon Zabaglione, *220,* 221–22
Rice
    Indian Chicken and Green Vegetable Pilau, 108–9
Rolls, Bourbon-Pecan and Coffee Sweet, *210,* 211–12

S

Salad dressing
    Umami in a Bottle, 18
Salads
    Crab and Crisp Apple, 180
    Farro and Crispy Kale, 63–64, *65*
    Green, A Different Kind of, 28, *29*
    Grilled Chicken, Southwestern, 102
    Peach, Sicilian-Style, *32,* 33
    Quinoa, *60,* 61–62
    Roasted Beet, *26, 27*
Salt, 10
Sandwiches
    Grilled Cheese, Broccoli and Kimchi, 82
    Grilled Cheese, Ham and Apple, 83
    Grilled Cheese, Spicy Kiwi and Bacon, 80, *81*
    Grilled Cheese, Ultimate, 79
    Nutella and Brown Butter Squash Panini, 232
    Ultimate BLT with "To-Mayo," 84–86, *85*
Seafood. *See* Crustaceans; Fish
Shortening, 8
Shrimp
    and Coconut Stew, Brazilian, 176, *177*
    Pasta, Creamy, with Charred Tomato and Pumpkin, 174–75
    Poached, Chilled Carrot Soup with, 171–73, *172*
Slaw, Coco-, 19
Smoke points, 7, 8
Soup, Chilled Carrot, with Poached Shrimp, 171–73, *172*
Sour flavors, 9
Soy sauce
    Umami in a Bottle, 18
Spinach
    Caesar Artichoke Dip, 39
Spreads
    Cherry-Olive Jam, 74
    To-Mayo, *85,* 86

Squash
    Brown Butter, and Nutella Panini,
        232
    Butternut, and Grilled Lobster with
        Tomato, Olive, and Preserved
        Lemon Relish, 181
    Butternut, Old Fashioned, Spiced,
        186
    Creamy Shrimp Pasta with Charred
        Tomato and Pumpkin, 174–75
    Pumpkin Pilaf, 46
    Skewers, 44, 45
    Spring Vegetable, Brown Butter, and
        Lemon Pasta, 52–54, 53
    Summer, Gratin, 48, 49
    Summer, Vongole, 66, 67
Stews
    Brazilian Shrimp and Coconut, 176,
        177
    Slow Cooker Sweet Potato and Ale
        Beef, 112–13
Sweet flavors, 11
Sweet Potato(es)
    and Ale Beef Stew, Slow Cooker,
        112–13
    Frico, aka Crispy Cheese Cakes, 87–
        89, 88
    Hash and Poblano, Fish with, 167
    Quinoa Salad, 60, 61–62

T
Toasts
    Avocado, 22, 23
    Lump Crab Bruschetta, 178, 179
    Watermelon Bruschetta, 30, 31
Tomato(es)
    Avocado "Succotash," 24, 25
    Charred, and Pumpkin, Creamy
        Shrimp Pasta with, 174–75
    Cherry, and Nectarine Crostata,
        206, 207–8
    Chicken Ragu, Creamy, 103–4, 105

Farro, Creamy, and Bacon, Fish with,
    154, 155
Lump Crab Bruschetta, 178, 179
Summer Squash Gratin, 48, 49
To-Mayo, 85, 86
Ultimate BLT with "To-Mayo," 84–
    86, 85
Vegetable Bolognese with Olive
    Gremolata, 70–71
Watermelon Bruschetta, 30, 31

U
Umami flavors, 10–11
Umami in a Bottle, 18

V
Vegetable(s). See also specific
    vegetables
    about, 16–17
Vodka
    Cucumber, Apple, and Sauvignon
        Blanc Sangria, 190, 191
    Peach, Basil, and Rosé Sangria, 192,
        193

W
Walnut and Olive Focaccia, 204–5
Watermelon Bruschetta, 30, 31
Whiskey
    Chocolate and Red Wine Bread
        Pudding, 233–35, 234
    Cocoa and Lemon Old Fashioned,
        185
Wine
    Cherry-Olive Jam, 74
    Chianti-Braised Beef with Grits,
        122–25, 123
    Cucumber, Apple, and Sauvignon
        Blanc Sangria, 190, 191
    Peach, Basil, and Rosé Sangria, 192,
        193
    Red, and Chocolate Bread Pudding,
        233–35, 234

Vernaccia-Poached Pears with
    Pecorino, 236, 237

Y
Yeast, 203

For information about permission to reproduce selections from this book, write
to trade.permissions@hmhco.com or to Permissions, Houghton Mifflin Harcourt
Publishing Company, 3 Park Avenue, 19th Floor, New York, New York 10016.

hmhbooks.com

Library of Congress Cataloging-in-Publication Data
Names: Briscione, James, 1980- author. | Parkhurst, Brooke, author. |
    Purcell, Andrew, 1978- photographer.
Title: Flavor for all : everyday recipes and creative pairings / James
    Briscione and Brooke Parkhurst ; photography by Andrew Purcell.
Description: Boston : Houghton Mifflin Harcourt, 2020. | Includes index. |
    Summary: "Simple, dynamic, flavor-packed recipes from the authors of The
    Flavor Matrix-informed by the science of flavor pairing but accessible
    enough for every cook"— Provided by publisher.
Identifiers: LCCN 2020016339 (print) | LCCN 2020016340 (ebook) | ISBN
    9780358164067 (hardback) | ISBN 9780358164029 (ebook)
Subjects: LCSH: Cooking. | Food—Composition. | Flavor. | LCGFT: Cookbooks.
Classification: LCC TX714 .B75336 2020 (print) | LCC TX714 (ebook) | DDC
    641.5--dc23
LC record available at https://lccn.loc.gov/2020016339
LC ebook record available at https://lccn.loc.gov/2020016340

Book design by Kara Plikaitis

Food styling by Carrie Purcell

Printed in China

SCP 10 9 8 7 6 5 4 3 2 1